Cambridge Elements

Elements in Critical Heritage Studies
edited by
Kristian Kristiansen
University of Gothenburg
Michael Rowlands
UCL

HEIRLOOM CULTURES AND HERITAGE BRANDING

The Creamy Case of Icelandic Skyr

Valdimar Tr. Hafstein
University of Iceland

Jón Þór Pétursson
University of Iceland

Photo editor:
Sigurlaug Dagsdóttir

Shaftesbury Road, Cambridge CB2 8EA, United Kingdom

One Liberty Plaza, 20th Floor, New York, NY 10006, USA

477 Williamstown Road, Port Melbourne, VIC 3207, Australia

314–321, 3rd Floor, Plot 3, Splendor Forum, Jasola District Centre, New Delhi – 110025, India

Cambridge University Press is part of Cambridge University Press & Assessment, a department of the University of Cambridge.

We share the University's mission to contribute to society through the pursuit of education, learning and research at the highest international levels of excellence.

www.cambridge.org
Information on this title: www.cambridge.org/9781009530323
DOI: 10.1017/9781009530286

© Valdimar Tr. Hafstein and Jón Þór Pétursson 2026

This publication is in copyright. Subject to statutory exception and to the provisions of relevant collective licensing agreements, no reproduction of any part may take place without the written permission of Cambridge University Press & Assessment.

When citing this work, please include a reference to the DOI 10.1017/9781009530286

First published 2026

A catalogue record for this publication is available from the British Library

A Cataloging-in-Publication data record for this Element is available from the Library of Congress

ISBN 978-1-009-53032-3 Hardback
ISBN 978-1-009-53029-3 Paperback
ISSN 2632-7074 (online)
ISSN 2632-7066 (print)

Cambridge University Press & Assessment has no responsibility for the persistence or accuracy of URLs for external or third-party internet websites referred to in this publication and does not guarantee that any content on such websites is, or will remain, accurate or appropriate.

For EU product safety concerns, contact us at Calle de José Abascal, 56, 1°, 28003 Madrid, Spain, or email eugpsr@cambridge.org

Heirloom Cultures and Heritage Branding

The Creamy Case of Icelandic Skyr

Elements in Critical Heritage Studies

DOI: 10.1017/9781009530286
First published online: February 2026

Valdimar Tr. Hafstein
University of Iceland

Jón Þór Pétursson
University of Iceland

Photo editor:
Sigurlaug Dagsdóttir

Authors for correspondence:
Valdimar Tr. Hafstein, vth@hi.is
Jón Þór Pétursson, jonthorp@hi.is

Abstract: Heritage branding and heirloom cultures are twin strategies for building brands in global markets. In this Element, the authors analyze these strategies through skyr: a traditional, sour dairy from Iceland. They explore how live microbial cultures in skyr have been "heritagized" as heirloom cultures to build a brand advantage. Live skyr cultures, they show, illustrate symbiotic relations over millennia between microbial cultures and human cultures. The industrialization of this species interaction in the twentieth and twenty-first centuries, they argue, ultimately converted a mutualistic relation into a parasitic one. Moreover, they demonstrate a parallel inversion of gender relations in the production and consumption of skyr as part of its industrialization and export. Ironically, these transformations undermine the industry's promotion of the cultures and heritage to which it has effectively put an end. They ask whether there is a more general lesson in this about the relationship between industrialization, capitalism, and heritage.

Keywords: cultural heritage, branding, ethnic fermented foods, gender, multispecies ethnography

© Valdimar Tr. Hafstein and Jón Þór Pétursson 2026

ISBNs: 9781009530323 (HB), 9781009530293 (PB), 9781009530286 (OC)
ISSNs: 2632-7074 (online), 2632-7066 (print)

Contents

1 Microbial Heritage and Cultural Contexts: Introduction   1

2 Heirloom Cultures   13

3 Heritage Branding   41

4 The Problematics of Cultural Heritage: Conclusions   67

   References   76

1 Microbial Heritage and Cultural Contexts: Introduction

In 2024, the French National Center for Scientific Research (CNRS) warned that Camembert and Brie may be on the brink of extinction. Their imminent demise is due to standardization of their production process over the past half century; through overly drastic selection, the food industry has severely diminished their genetic and microbial diversity (Harmi, 2024). The traditional method for making Camembert was to age the cheese in damp caves, in which the fungi responsible for creating the famous rind exist naturally. This environmental microbiome gave each batch of Camembert its distinctive character. The result of a symbiotic relation: farmers fed the fungi and bacteria with dairy and were rewarded with rindy cheese in various colors and tastes (a little redder, a little bluer, a little greyer, or a little whiter) (Lederman and Sowden, 2024).

In the twentieth century, however, consumers increasingly developed a taste for white rind. To meet their demand, producers started to engineer the process and produce the fungi in a lab. They isolated a specific albino strain that became known as Penicillium Camemberti. This fungus created the perfect white rind for which Camembert and Brie are known. As cheesemakers the world over adopted this strain, it brought the desired consistency to these cheeses. But slowly it endangered their microbial diversity. As a result, over time, Penicillium Camemberti has lost some of its ability to reproduce naturally and scientists have reverted to using asexual reproduction to grow the fungi. A long-term concern is that such an isolated strain is susceptible to a pathogen or a disease that could wipe out the entire fungi population (Lederman and Sowden, 2024). Biological diversity is a natural defense against extinction.

The dire prognosis for the beloved French cheeses illustrates Ricardo Rozzi's decade-old warning that "biocultural homogenization" is the main "global driver of losses of biological and cultural diversity" (2013, p. 9). Along the same line, anthropologist Thomas Hylland Eriksen (2021) has argued that homogenization and standardization as central features of modernity are disastrous for biological and cultural diversity. Others have claimed that as a result, the world is witnessing a sixth extinction in nature (Kolbert, 2014).

1.1 Probiotic Microbiopolitics

In a pungent ethnography of artisanal raw-milk cheese making in the United States, Heather Paxson coined the term "microbiopolitics" to refer to the "creation of categories of microscopic biological agents; the anthropocentric evaluation of such agents; and the elaboration of appropriate human behaviors vis-à-vis microorganisms engaged in infection, inoculation, and digestion" (Paxson, 2008, p. 17). The age of microbiopolitics began with Louis Pasteur's

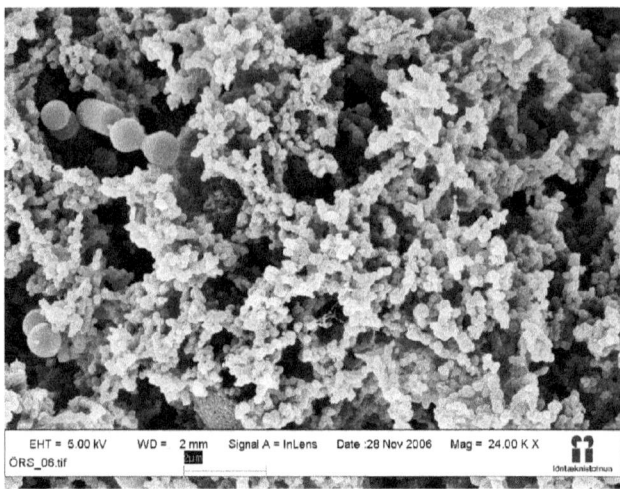

Figure 1 A microscopic view of skyr microbes showing bead-chains of Streptococcus thermophilus and a few sticks of Lactobacillus bulgaricus. Photograph by Jón Matthíasson. Courtesy of Guðmundur Guðmundsson, Rheology and Microstructure of Skyr. M.Sc. thesis, University of Iceland, 2007.

research on fermentation and immunology in the second half of the nineteenth century and the subsequent ascendancy of "Pasteurianism" as an ethical and legal regime in the fields of food production and medicine (Figure 1). Referring to the artisans with whom she worked as "today's post-Pasteurians," Paxson remarks that through their fermentation practices they "seek to rescue indigenous cultures – microbial but also human – from industrial homogeneity" (Paxson, 2008, p. 23).

As people increasingly come to see microbes as allies to be nurtured rather than foes to be exterminated, researchers have sought to describe an emergent post-Pasteurian point of view, from which human–microbial symbiosis is not centered in the "wars on germs" of the twentieth century (cf. Latour, 1993; Otis, 2000; Sinsheimer, 2018). Instead, based in an understanding of ourselves as ecological creatures this perspective brings into focus the beneficial effects of the "human microbiome" (Gilbert et al., 2012; Helmreich, 2014 and 2015; Sangodeyi, 2014; Wahlqvist, 2016). Increasingly, microbes are portrayed as potent and omnipresent actors that have the power not only to harm but also to sustain humanity (Velasquez-Manoff, 2012; Yong, 2016). A paradigm shift is underway: rather than seeing microbes as inherently bad (pathogenic) or good (beneficial), a growing body of research has moved on from a narrow focus on germ theory – that certain diseases are caused by the invasion of the discrete body by foreign microorganisms – to broader ecological understanding of human–microbial relationships, incorporating socioeconomic, cultural, spatial, and political contexts (Benezra, 2020; Benezra et al., 2012; Ironstone, 2019; Tracy and Howes-Mischel, 2018; Paxson, 2008, 2014a and 2019; Sarmiento, 2020).

At the same time, increasing scientific knowledge of the role of microbes in promoting human health and wellness has given rise to new expectations and values that are increasingly commodified and contested (Blaser, 2014; Bloomfield, 2016; Chuong et al., 2017; Greenhough et al., 2020; Hawkins and O'Doherty, 2011; Lorimer, 2016; Rhodes et al., 2013; Wolf-Meyer, 2017). This might be described as a probiotic turn in the social imagination as well as in the food and health industries. Rising interest among the public in gut health is mirrored in the growth of the global probiotics market; market analysts estimate its value somewhere between 80 and 90 billion US dollars in 2024 and forecast between 100 percent and 200 percent growth in market size over the next five to seven years (Probiotics Market Size, 2024). That market includes probiotic foods and beverages, on the one hand, and dietary supplements, on the other (Figure 2).

Directly ingesting microbes through supplements is a novelty, to be sure. Consuming probiotic foods and drinks, on the other hand, is certainly not novel. Fermentation is an ancient and widespread method for transforming and conserving food. Since the agricultural revolution over ten thousand years ago, the

Figure 2 MS Dairy skyr commercial. Courtesy of MS Iceland Dairies.

fermentation of foods and beverages has been essential to people's diets in most societies (El Sheikha and Hu, 2020; Katz, 2011 and 2012; Ray and Joshi, 2014; Tamang et al., 2020). From sauerkraut to sourdough, from kimchi to miso, from beer to kombucha, from yogurt to cheese, many traditional foods and drinks in societies across Europe and worldwide are produced through fermentation by live cultures. The live cultures involved comprise diverse species of bacteria, fungi, and other microorganisms that co-habit the earth with human and non-human animals and plants. Indeed, traditional fermented foods and drinks are prime examples of biocultural heritage, ecosystems that result from long-term social and biological relationships between humans, other animals, plants, soils, and microbes (Lorimer, 2016 and 2020; Lyons, 2020). These relationships have shaped human health, memory, practices, and traditional knowledge. Taken together, fermented foods may thus be described as "a key reservoir of microbial diversity in the human diet" (Hernández-Velázquez et al., 2024).

1.2 Original Skyr

One such fermented food is skyr, a thick and sour dairy product. Outside of Iceland, it is often referred to as a thick yogurt but technically it is an acid-curd cheese. Skyr played a large role in sustaining the Icelandic population from the era of settlement in the 800–900s CE and up to the present day. Until the twentieth century, most people in Iceland lived from subsistence farming with grass as the major crop and dairying a major occupation. Animal products provided the bulk of people's daily food, with dairy accounting for an important proportion (Gísladóttir, 1999; Júlíusson, 2013). Most of that dairy took the form of skyr, for skyr making was a way to preserve the 90 percent that remains of fresh milk after the cream has been skimmed off and churned into butter. Skyr is produced by heating skimmed milk, then cooling it again before adding live fermentative microbial cultures, which effectively make the skyr by curdling the milk. Traditionally, the fermentative cultures came from a pinch of skyr from the previous batch, deliberately conserved for this purpose. After culturing and coagulating, skyr is strained to remove the watery whey, making the final product creamy and rich in texture.

Skyr might be defined as an ecosystem created and sustained by relations between Streptococcus and Lactobacillus bacteria, various yeast species (Valsdóttir et al., 2011; Valsdóttir and Sveinsson, 2011), mammals such as cows, sheep, or goats, their pastures and soils, as well as the humans who tend to them and eat them. The live cultures of skyr provide an excellent case study of symbiosis between microbial cultures and human cultures through their respective histories. Indeed, the long-term resilience and adaptation of the skyr

Figure 3 Through the centuries in Iceland, humans, animals and microbes lived in symbiosis in turf houses, contributing to a diverse skyr microbiome. Photograph by Hannes Pálsson. Courtesy of the National Museum of Iceland.

microbiome, along with its natural and cultural selection over time, fostered great microbial diversity. As a result, skyr microbes make up a unique part of ecological diversity in Iceland (Figure 3).

In a twist that is reminiscent of the development and fate of Brie and Camembert, however, standardization, hygiene regulation, and technological innovations in skyr production have greatly impoverished its microbial diversity over the past one hundred years. The formerly diverse microbiome of traditional skyr in Iceland has been reduced to a single strain of one single microbial species, cloned for large-scale industrial production in a multinational biochemical factory. The story of skyr, like that of its French cousins, is thus the story of missing microbes in modern industrial and postindustrial societies. That story recounts a crucial dimension of the loss of biodiversity in our era as microbes are the dominant form of life on the planet: microbes make up two-thirds of life on earth and, indeed, more than half the cells of the human body (Yong, 2016). Ironically, the single strain cloned for industrial production has been trademarked as "Original Icelandic Skyr Cultures" in the European dairy market and as "Heirloom Icelandic Skyr Cultures" in the US dairy market.

1.3 Heirlooms and Monocultures

There is good reason to take a step back and consider the implications. The term "heirloom" in "heirloom cultures" is inspired by concepts like "heirloom seeds" and "heirloom tomatoes." By the middle of the twentieth century, agriculture in North America, and to a growing extent elsewhere, turned "away from a broader array of crops based on open pollination towards a narrow range of hybrid crops" (Jordan, 2007, p. 28). Large-scale industrial production resorted where possible to mechanical harvesting, but as Carolyn de la Peña remarks in an essay on "the mechanized tomato," "no existing varieties could withstand the violence of mechanical cutting, separating, sorting, and loading" (de la Peña, 2013, p. 35). Since flavor was not a characteristic that influenced mechanical compatibility, it became no more than an afterthought in the breeding of the perfect tomato. Instead, industrial-scale agriculture bred for consistency, durability, longevity, visual appearance, and transport across distances without significant damage. As a result, while transportation allowed access to produce out of season, the varieties available to consumers decreased dramatically.

Meanwhile, older varieties – over 3,000 of them – were still grown at small scale in "the backyards of tomato fanatics and solitary seed savers," as Jennifer A. Jordan notes in her investigation of "The Heirloom Tomato as Cultural Object" (Jordan, 2007, p. 21). The term "heirloom" began to be used to describe these varieties in the 1980s and 1990s: varieties that predate the rise of industrial agriculture, can be pollen fertilized, and have a history of their own. The "heirloom tomato" found its way back to the dining table through farmers' markets and community-supported agriculture in North America and Europe. In the context of organic farming and an appeal for traditional, natural foods over industrial foods and monocultures, it eventually staged a seasonal return to restaurants and grocery stores. Unlike typical grocery store tomatoes bred for uniformity and durability, heirlooms come in a wide range of colors and have rich, complex flavors (Jordan, 2007; Joseph et al., 2017).

By the turn of the twenty-first century, heirloom tomatoes and seeds had popularized the term "heirloom" among foodies. It was a short step, then, to describe fermentation cultures as heirlooms to emphasize their lineage, resilience, and the artistry involved in maintaining them over time. With implicit reference to conceptions of biocultural heritage, the term "heirloom cultures" has thus over the past quarter-century come to describe the traditional agents in the fermentation of skyr, yogurt, kefir, and other fermented dairy products. Its use signals the affirmation of heritage values such as authenticity and presence.

The revival of microbial heritage, or heirloom cultures, coincides with the rise of the Slow Food movement in the 1990s and 2000s, a growing interest in

Figure 4 Skyr was traditionally stored in wooden barrels where microbes soured and preserved skyr for the winter season. Photograph by Hans Kuhn. Courtesy of the National Museum of Iceland.

traditional food preparation since the turn of the century, and rising awareness of gut health in the past decade. Typically, the term heirloom cultures describes fermentation cultures preserved over generations, cherished for their flavors, fermentation characteristics, and probiotic qualities. Just as heirloom seeds are kept for their distinctive traits, heirloom cultures are maintained for their time-tested characteristics that cannot easily be replicated with mass-produced starters. Each culture can carry specific strains of bacteria and yeast that give foods distinctive textures and flavors, which commercial, mass-produced starters often lack (Figure 4). A preference for heirloom cultures can also signal a commitment to microbial diversity over the monocultural values of scale and productivity. The dairy industry's trademarking of "Heirloom Skyr Cultures" thus appears to appropriate a commitment to biocultural diversity for the purposes of branding a commercial dairy product produced with standardized, monoculture strains selected for consistency, shelf-stability, and efficiency. One might describe this move as a capture of language, or perhaps as ironic branding, designed to suggest time-depth and artisanal authenticity, even in their absence.

1.4 Lactobacillus, Sour Milk, and Superfood

In 1904, a young Bulgarian physician named Stamen Grigoroff began his work to isolate the microorganisms that played the key role in fermenting sour milk. Grigoroff worked with samples taken from his native village Studen Izvor, whose inhabitants were known throughout Bulgaria for good health and longevity. Grigoroff discovered three different microorganisms in Bulgarian sour milk ("Kissélo-mléko"), which he named *Bacille A*, *Microcoque B*, and *Streptobacille C*. It was *Bacille A*, he found, that causes milk to curdle, transforming it into yogurt; it soon came to be called *Lactic acid bacillus* or *Lactobacillus*. The particular strain of Lactobacillus that Grigoroff discovered was later named Bacillus Bulgaricus in his honor. *Microcoque B* came to be known as *Streptococcus thermophilus*. Grigoroff isolated these three species and was able to ferment milk with each one, with vastly different outcomes in taste and texture. When he mixed his three samples of fermented milk together, however, the three species resumed their symbiosis, and the outcome once again resembled the original Bulgarian sour milk with which the experiment began (Grigoroff, 1905; Nancheva, 2019; Stoilova, 2015).

At the Pasteur Institute in Paris, the Russian biologist Elie Metchnikoff had already built a reputation for his research into the biology of aging as well as of gut microbiota. He invited Grigoroff to Paris to speak to his colleagues about his discoveries. A couple of years later, Metchnikoff built on Grigoroff's findings in his hypothesis that regular consumption of yogurt and other fermented milk could positively influence the intestinal micro-flora and promote good health and longevity. Metchnikoff took particular interest in the longevity of Bulgarian villagers and attributed it to the large quantity of lactic acid bacteria that they consumed in their daily bowl of yogurt. Moreover, Metchnikoff conducted several experiments along with his lab assistants and found that not all *Lactic acid bacillus* were created equal. Bulgarian bacilli, he found, were most beneficial to the intestinal micro-flora (Stoilova, 2015).

In 1905, Metchnikoff gave a public lecture in Paris in which he argued that harmful intestinal bacteria contribute to aging and that eating yogurt and other fermented dairy helps to cultivate beneficial bacteria to counteract "intestinal putrefaction" and its effects on the body. His lecture made headlines on both sides of the Atlantic and sparked an international "yogurt mania." Not only did the production and consumption of Bulgarian-style yogurt spread across the European and North-American continents; pharmacies also sold "Bulgarian cultures in the form of tablets, powders, and boullions – precursors of today's probiotics" (Vikhanski, 2016).

Metchnikoff published his findings in two influential volumes: *Scientifically Sour Milk: Its Influence in Arresting Intestinal Putrefaction* (1996[1907]) and *The Prolongation of Life: Optimistic Studies* (2004[1908]). The latter was translated into English in 1908, the same year as he was awarded the Nobel Prize for his research into immunology, aging, and microorganisms. His work kicked off a new era in microbiology as scientists set out to explore the relationship between microbiota and intestinal health. It also provided a scientific rationale to the belief that regular consumption of yogurt promotes good health and combats aging (Yotova, 2018). A superfood was born.

Some few years after the publication of Metchnikoff's books, knowledge of the benefits of sour milk had reached Icelandic shores. Gísli Guðmundsson was the first Icelandic microbiologist, educated at various European universities from 1910 to 1913. Upon returning to Iceland, one of his first projects was a study of the microbiology of skyr. He published the results in 1914 in *Búnaðarritið* ("Journal of Agriculture"), where he accounts for the various bacteria and fungi discovered in traditional skyr. Having summarized Metchnikoff's work on fermented dairy, Guðmundsson focused in particular on his findings about the health benefits of *Streptococcus thermophilus*. Relying on the observations of Metchnikoff and Grigoroff, he also posed the question which is healthier: freshly made skyr or older skyr. Guðmundsson concluded that freshly made skyr might be healthier due to the diminishing effect of skyr cultures over time. His principal argument rests on a comparison with the eating habits of Bulgarians: they make and consume their yogurt daily, which explains their good health and longevity. It bears noting in this context that Guðmundsson was working with timescales that belonged to Icelandic peasant society, not to shelf-life in our days of "best before" stamps: by "older" he referred to more than six months old; skyr was "new" until it reached that respectable age. In his article from 1914, Guðmundsson moreover reports success in isolating clear skyr cultures that closely resembled Bulgarian yogurt cultures. He even managed to mix the two together to make "sour milk": Icelandic-Bulgarian microbial cooperation at its finest. Guðmundsson also noted that people all over the world make products similar to skyr. The most well-known, he wrote, is "the Bulgarian skyr," a.k.a. yogurt; other skyr-like foods, he adds, from other parts of the world include kefir, matzoon, and kumis. Seeing as in recent years, skyr is often labeled Icelandic-style yogurt in global dairy markets, Guðmundsson's enumeration of skyr-like products from other regions, including "Bulgarian-style skyr," may serve to remind us of the global diversity of fermented dairies and their traditional microbiomes.

In the first decades of the twentieth century, Bulgaria and its healthy, long-lived inhabitants were ubiquitous in the marketing of this exoticized superfood in Europe and the United States. As a result, Bulgarian yogurt became synonymous with all yogurt-like products. It ceased to matter very much whether any given yogurt was produced in Bulgaria. Instead, what came to matter was the general association between Bulgarianness, good health, and longevity, all neatly packaged in a cup of yogurt – without regard to where it was actually produced or packaged.

Of course, international success did not go unnoticed in the homeland of this life elixir. Elitsa Stoilova has examined the "Bulgarianization" of yogurt making in Bulgaria in the first half of the twentieth century. Stoilova points out that the large-scale commercialization of yogurt demanded standardization of the production process. At its outset, as in the case of skyr in Iceland, most households in Bulgaria still made their own yogurt. Indeed, as Lindsey Foltz remarks in her ethnography of "Microbial Entanglements in the Bulgarian Cellar," home production of yogurt and other fermented foods is still widespread in the Bulgarian countryside (Foltz, 2024). In the first half of the twentieth century, even as regional dairies began to expand and standardize their production, there were still considerable regional differences regarding the taste, texture, and microbial composition of Bulgarian yogurt. As late as the 1930s, dairies in the capital Sofia used diverse starter cultures and worked under different sanitary conditions. This lack of standardization worried Bulgarian dairy scientists who were alarmed that various dairies were allowed to produce yogurt with different tastes and textures (Figure 5).

To counter this inconsistency, dairy scientists advocated for improved sanitary control. They also introduced "clear cultures" instead of the traditional "maya" (the starter culture) (Stoilova, 2013). Bulgarian yogurt ought only to

Figure 5 Laboratory in a dairy cooperative in 1930. The industrialization of skyr was accompanied by scientific research that aimed to enhance and standardize the traditional dairy. Photograph by Magnús Ólafsson. Courtesy of the Reykjavík Museum of Photography.

contain the microorganisms *Lactobacillus bulgaricus* and *Streptococcus thermophilus*, studied by Grigoroff and Metchnikoff. This meant that any yogurt produced with other, unspecified microorganisms should be considered uncharacteristic for Bulgarian yogurt. Through standardization of the microbiome, Bulgarian scientists thus helped to define Bulgarian yogurt as a national product. First, by getting rid of the traditional starter culture with its environmental microbiomes, the yogurt was delocalized. Then, adding instead the same clear cultures in every Bulgarian dairy the yogurt was relocalized, now as a national product. Standardized within the state borders, Stoilova concludes that by "establishing common characteristics, the experts transformed yogurt into Bulgarian yogurt: a product with its own specifications and production technology" (Stoilova, 2013, p. 75). Bulgaria as the homeland of yogurt thus became a locus of ethno-national authenticity at the microbial level.

1.5 Optimal Compositions and Exclusive Rights

Although Icelandic consumers were only introduced to yogurt in the late 1960s, similar trends prevailed in the Icelandic dairy industry through the twentieth century regarding the standardization of production and regimentation of the microbiome. Throughout the century, Icelandic scientists and dairy managers made every effort to standardize the production of skyr to eliminate all differences in microbial composition, taste, and texture. Biologists and dairy scientists joined hands to determine the optimal microbial composition in skyr and set about eliminating all "non-essential" microbes in the process. We recount that story in the following section, but we set it in the Bulgarian context here for it is important to remark that almost no aspect of the story of skyr is unique or without counterparts elsewhere: from the standardization of cultures to the safeguarding of heirloom cultures and cultural heritage (in a double sense); and from notions of local microbial "terroir" to heritage branding for global markets. On the contrary, the story of skyr offers a particularly rich case study in processes of heritagization, in particular for food heritage but also for cultural heritage more broadly conceived.

Of course, such comparisons run in more than one direction. Thus, for example, the twenty-first century has witnessed increasing efforts to reframe various forms of cultural heritage in terms of intellectual property. The patenting of genetic resources, from seeds to microbes, has caused controversy, generating debates and diplomatic negotiations at the international level. Likewise, the trademark regime has been invoked at national and international levels to protect traditional products or create competitive advantage in global markets. Staying with the comparative case of yogurt, in 2002 Bulgarian delegates demanded protection for yogurt labeling at a meeting of the World Trade Organization in Geneva. Their aim was to prevent producers outside Bulgaria from labeling their dairy as Bulgarian yogurt or "Bulgarian-style." The Bulgarian delegates thus contested the prevailing understanding that the Agreement on Trade-Related Aspects of Intellectual Property Rights (TRIPS) from 1994 allows any global producer to label their yogurts as Bulgarian or Bulgarian-style yogurt. French producers vehemently opposed the demands of the Bulgarian delegates. They had long labeled their yogurts as Bulgarian or Bulgarian-style, they argued, on the understanding that these were generic, descriptive terms, referencing a kind of product, like Arabic coffee or Indian curry, rather than the country of production (Stoilova, 2015). To cut a long story short, the Bulgarian demand did not carry the day.

Shortly thereafter, the dairy company MS Iceland Dairies attempted to register the term "skyr" as a trademark to protect its production against foreign competitors in the global dairy market and claim exclusive rights to market its dairy products as skyr. Another attempt that failed, as we recount further on. We will also show that in response to this setback, the principal producer of Icelandic skyr developed an alternative game plan to build its brand. Two-pronged, its strategy involved, on the one hand, branding skyr as cultural heritage in its labels, packaging, PR, and advertising, even going so far as to build a skyr museum in Iceland as a local anchor for its global exports, and, on the other hand, presenting its skyr as a product of authentic Icelandic heirloom cultures, which could be both certified and trademarked.

1.6 The Case of Icelandic Skyr

In the twenty-first century, skyr has transformed from an everyday staple to national food heritage and global superfood. International fame is perhaps the crowning moment in the historical trajectory of this humble food. Iceland MS Dairies, the principal dairy company in Iceland, now exports its skyr to thirteen countries and counting, competing with other thick dairy products marketed as skyr by global dairy conglomerates. These include the three dairy giants – Lactalis, Nestlé, and Danone – as well as Arla Foods and innumerable smaller competitors. Most of them refer to Icelandic nature, culture, and history to market their skyr (or "Icelandic-style yogurt"). In comparison, MS Iceland Dairies has a relatively limited share on the global dairy market but positions itself vis-à-vis the competition by underlining the origin and cultural authenticity of its product.

As emerges from the creamy example of skyr, heritage branding and heirloom cultures are twin strategies for building brands in global markets. We analyze these strategies through the story of a traditional, sour dairy from Iceland that has recently carved out a place in the dairy aisle of supermarkets across the world. We explore how microbial cultures have been "heritagized" as heirloom cultures to build a brand advantage in the global dairy trade. Delving into their history, we find that live skyr cultures may serve to illustrate symbiotic relations over millennia between microbial cultures and human cultures. We examine the correlation between the industrialization of this species interaction in the twentieth and twenty-first centuries and the simultaneous rise to prominence of heirloom cultures and heritage branding as marketing strategies. Industrialization also reversed traditional gender roles in the production of skyr, subordinating women in the dairy or pushing them altogether out of this formerly female-dominated space; the international branding of skyr, however, celebrates the women who safeguarded the tradition and the cultures through the centuries for present-day consumers. The marketing campaigns imagine these consumers as superwomen who buy superfood, transfiguring women as producers into women as consumers.

We ask whether there are more general lessons in all of this about cultural heritage and its relationship to capitalism. We return to that question in the conclusions, as we examine in retrospect the trajectory of skyr from cultural diversity to cloned microbial monoculture and bring into focus the logic by which the final part of this trajectory has reframed microbes as heirloom cultures, transformed skyr into cultural heritage superfood, and reimagined women as its consumers rather than its producers. From live cultures to cultural heritage, we argue that the story of skyr and its transformations raises important questions about heritage branding and about cultural heritage as a product, a destination, and a consumer good.

2 Heirloom Cultures

> Once upon a time, 1,100 years ago in fact, Nordic settlers began arriving in Iceland. They brought with them the skills and knowledge for producing skyr. As time passed, the know-how and recipe for this nutritious food slowly faded out elsewhere in the Nordic region. Luckily, the Icelandic skyr making tradition continued.
>
> For centuries, Icelandic skyr formed a cornerstone of the national diet, helping to keep people strong in living conditions that were often harsh. On family farms countrywide, it was the women who nurtured this dairy and passing on [sic] both the recipe and the original Icelandic skyr cultures from mother to daughter.
>
> (Ísey skyr, 2025)

With near monopoly in the domestic market, MS Iceland Dairies, in 2017, began promoting a new brand of skyr to better distinguish its product on the global dairy shelf: Ísey skyr. The company's advertisements introduce Ísey as a beautiful Icelandic female name; the name refers both to ice ("ís") and to the island ("ey"), referencing Iceland itself in the guise of a woman. The lids of plastic skyr buckets sold in supermarkets across Europe assure consumers that "Ísey Skyr is a remarkable dairy product unique to Iceland" (a claim apparently undermined by the small print on some of these buckets that denotes the country of origin as Denmark – much like Arla's skyr).

Skyr is thus anchored in the past, the know-how and recipe handed down from one generation to the next for centuries, even millennia, from mother to daughter, as the advertising explains: "It was some of these very same women, the recipients of their mother's expertise, who, around 90 years ago, taught Icelandic dairy scientists the art of skyr-making" (Ísey skyr, 2025). Historically, the dairy was indeed a domain of female authority and female labor. Thanks to geographical isolation, the tradition of skyr making was safeguarded in Iceland in contrast to other countries in Northern Europe, in which it may once have been quotidian but is now a long-lost art. In other words, this is a story of cultural resilience – in more ways than one, for skyr making depends not only on the survival of cultural tradition but no less so on the resilience of traditional microbial cultures. As MS Dairies claims, "the basic recipe and the use of original cultures to ferment the skimmed milk remain the same" (Ísey skyr, 2025). The opening formula of "The Ísey Skyr Story" quoted above suggests that the survival of skyr is a sort of modern fairy tale: "once upon a time." If that is so, the skyr microbiome plays the protagonist role and Icelandic women that of fairy godmother. The tale begins when the microbes leave home and set sail for Iceland along with their human helpers.

Skyr is high in protein and low in fat, and its nutritional value accounts for its newfound international success within a low-fat, high-protein consumer culture. But it has a long history, one that can be traced through written sources and archeological records back to the first millennium, though it is probably considerably older. Culinary historian and folklorist Hallgerður Gísladóttir's scholarship on food traditions (1999) is the go-to source for an understanding of skyr making in Iceland's traditional peasant society. A static society in many respects, there is not much evidence to show any developments in the making of skyr from the age of Iceland's settlement in the 800s until the beginning of the twentieth century. Milking was women's work and so was the production of butter, skyr, and whey from the milk. When the milk settles in its containers, the cream floats to the top. Once it was skimmed off, the cream was churned into butter – the best way to conserve it. Due to lack of firewood, salt was always in short supply in Iceland; adapting to this, butter was usually cultured (or soured) for conservation (Gísladóttir, 1999, p. 65). Butter was currency; according to eighteenth-century sources it could be preserved for over twenty years (Halldórsson, [1783]1973; Ólafsson and Pálsson, 1975). In addition to contributing labor, tenant farmers often paid rent in butter; landowners would collect – and eat – butter, it could be exchanged for other goods, and merchant and laborers' wages could even be paid in butter. Accounts from the late sixteenth century of the diocese of Hólar, a major landholder in the north of Iceland, show that the bishop owned a mountain of butter weighing up to forty tons, much of it rent for church-owned lands (Tómasson, 2016, p. 119–121).

However, for each liter of cream skimmed off the top of milk and churned into butter, nine liters of skimmed milk are left over. Skimmed milk, in other words, is a byproduct of butter-making. To make skyr was to add value to this byproduct and to preserve it before the invention of refrigeration. It also improved both taste and texture. At room temperature, skimmed milk could become both bitter and unsafe within a few days; heating milk and/or replacing bad microbial cultures with good ones is one of the more important innovations of pre-industrial food safety technology (Jönsson, 2005).

From Iceland's settlement in the ninth century and through the seventeenth century, work at the dairy also included making cheese but that art fell victim to natural catastrophe in the eighteenth century (Gísladóttir, 1999). Following decades of miserable weather, landfast ice on the coastline, and small hay harvests, the greatest eruption since settlement sent volcanic ash and toxic fumes over most of the country, its aftereffects killing more than 60 percent of the livestock within a year, causing widespread famine (followed by pestilence) in which ca. 20 percent of the population perished (Hálfdanarson, 1984; Rafnsson 1984). A contemporary account in a farming guide from the end of the eighteenth century notes that "Cheese is made from the same material as skyr, but in the current circumstances for farming in the country, every provident housewife will see that skyr making will supply more food than cheese making, particularly as there is now so little livestock following hard years and hay shortage" (quoted in Sigurðardóttir, 1985, p. 242). During these "hard years," the necessary traditional know-how seems to have been lost; cheese making did not resume until much later under foreign influence.

When making skyr, women would (often but not always) begin by heating the skimmed milk. This was pre-Pasteurian dairying, so the goal in heating the milk was not to kill unwanted microbes but rather to make the skyr smooth instead of grainy. Heating denatures the proteins, which helps the cultures to bind them together later in the process. The milk would then be cooled down again before adding a pinch of skyr from the previous batch, which contained the skyr cultures. A pinch of skyr contained various species of fermentative bacteria and yeasts, and served as an inoculum from a previous, successful skyr making.

This is known as "backslopping" and is common practice in the fermentation of milk all over the world, where people "use old batches of whey or yogurt to inoculate a new production with a stable and safe microbial community" (Reichhardt et al., 2021, p. S345).

For the best outcome, it was important to inoculate the new batch of skyr with a healthy balanced microbiome. These cultures set to work in the skimmed milk, beginning a fermentative process that leads to acidification, by which milk becomes skyr; the bacteria and yeast feed on lactose, producing lactic acid as a waste product. Lactic acid inhibits the growth of microbes that might otherwise spoil the milk. In many cases, skyr makers also added rennet, an enzymatic agent to facilitate coagulation; usually a piece of a newly slaughtered calf's or lamb's stomach, which helps the skyr thicken and settle into its ready, semi-solid state. Finally, after it had cooled down again, skyr makers strained the skyr through cloth using one of a variety of traditional straining devices. That last step separated the whey from the skyr. Every cup of skyr leaves roughly three cups of whey as a byproduct. Indeed, the name refers to this separation; etymologically, skyr is related to the Icelandic verb "skera," to cut or divide, which in turn is a close relative of modern English "shear."

In Iceland, skyr has long been a household staple that is eaten on its own, mixed with porridge, served with whey, or eaten with cream for festive occasions. Berries picked in August were sometimes conserved in skyr for the autumn months. As there was little cereal cultivation in Iceland and firewood was scarce, skyr was eaten when bread and porridge might have been served in other countries. The fermented whey that the straining of skyr left over was likewise an everyday beverage mixed with water, the only alternative to a glass of water for most days of the year. As cereals had to be imported, beer was only consumed on festive occasions. But whey was also an important conservation medium, an alternative to salt, which was always in short supply. All sorts of meat and offal were pickled in whey, the great acidity of which had the added benefit of softening even the toughest foods (Gísladóttir, 1999; Sigurðardóttir, 1985; Pétursdóttir, 1960).

Each household made its own skyr, producing and conserving the live cultures needed to make the dairy product. To make a new batch of skyr, it was necessary to preserve a bit of skyr from the previous batch. Skyr was mostly a seasonal food made during summertime, especially in connection with the weaning of lambs (and kids and calves) which traditionally took place near the end of June (Figure 6). This meant that women often had to borrow microbial cultures, a pinch of old skyr, that is, from a neighboring household that had managed to preserve the cultures the whole year, or else make them again from fresh milk (Pétursdóttir 1960, p. 14). The resilience and adaptation of the skyr microbiome, its natural and

Figure 6 Milking cows and making dairy foods was in the hands of Icelandic women from the time of settlement well into the twentieth century. Photograph by Guðmundur G. Bárðarson. Courtesy of the National Museum of Iceland.

cultural selection, fostered microbial diversity. The first Icelandic microbiologist (or bacteriologist, as the profession was known at the time), Gísli Guðmundsson, studied the microbial composition of skyr in the 1910s and found that in addition to *Streptococcus thermophilus* bacteria, skyr contained various yeast and mold fungi, such as *Torula*, *Mycoderma*, *Monilia Candida*, and *Oidium Lactis* (Guðmundsson, 1914, p. 11). Indeed, bacteriologist Sigurður Pétursson noted in the 1930s that "Skyr making literally is the breeding of certain bacterial species and therefore a complicated task" (Pétursson, 1939).

2.1 Symbiosis

The live microbial cultures of traditional skyr and their reproduction in the dairy provide a prime example of symbiosis between microbial cultures and human cultures or, to put it differently, of species interaction between microbes and humans: collaborative cultural practices. Indeed, in the past two decades we have learned to understand the human organism as a "composite of many species" (Paxson, 2008, p. 38–39); the numbers vary a bit but by all accounts "we" are outnumbered; that is, less than half of our bodies' cells are human (ca. 1:1.3), the majority consisting of a multitude of microbial species with whom we coexist in the most intimate way imaginable, co-consuming and co-producing (Sender et al., 2016a and 2016b). As Donna Haraway has taught us, being human is to be more-than-human, it is to "become with" other species with whom we share life: "to be one is always to become with many (Haraway, 2008, p. 4). In other words (those of environmental geographer Jamie Lorimer), to be human is "a multispecies achievement" dependent on the "generosity of microbial life" (Lorimer, 2016, p. 58).

Certain microbes, including those in skyr, have played a key role over millennia in the development of the genetic ability to digest milk in adulthood among some human populations (Rosenstock et al., 2021). Known as lactase persistence, this ability is historically related to pastoral agriculture and is today strongest and most widespread among northern European populations (Gerbault et al., 2011). However, recent studies indicate that it was still relatively rare in Europe as late as the Bronze Age (3000–1000 BCE), suggesting that it developed only in the last 3,000 years (Allentoft et al., 2015). Lactase persistence is a textbook case of how microbes have shaped not only human culture but also the human gut, highlighting human–microbe hybridity (Ingram, 2011) and how microbes have co-evolved with human culture and human genes. As Edwin Sayes notes, "nonhumans do not have agency by themselves, if only because they are never by themselves" (Sayes, 2014, p. 144), but of course the same may be said of humans – as is evident in the history of skyr making. Agency between humans and nonhumans – skyr microbes included – is thus best described as relational, spun between social actors (Barad, 2003; Whatmore, 2002, p. 4).

Fermentation is an excellent example of this relationality. While approximately 40 trillion bacterial cells within the human body are busy fermenting at any given moment – protecting tissues, regulating the immune system, and nourishing cells – fermentation also forms an integral part of traditional foodways across the world. In fermenting these foods, people effectively create "an extended microbiome, an externalization and functional expansion of the metabolic processes carried out within our own bodies" (Dunn et al., 2020; Hendy et al., 2021, p. 197).

Historical and archeological records attest to the consumption of skyr in the first centuries after Iceland's settlement in the ninth century CE, accounting for more than a third (maybe more) of the period in which lactase persistence may have evolved. What is perhaps most interesting about traditional skyr making is that there seems to have been no standardized way of doing it, no more than there were standard skyr microbes. There were important regional differences in producing and sustaining the microbial cultures, both in terms of ingredients and methods, and even skyr making equipment could differ from one household to the next (Gísladóttir, 1999). Since most households made skyr, skyr inevitably came in different forms.

Differences in microbial cultures, production methods, and equipment also meant that the taste and texture of skyr varied between regions and even households. Not only that, skyr was made from whatever milk was available, which, in keeping with the livestock, was most usually sheep's milk, often cow's milk, more rarely goat's milk. This much we learn from otherwise scarce historical records. The taste and texture of skyr is determined to a large extent by the kind of microbial flora that becomes dominant in the milk when it curdles; this depends in turn on the composition (how skimmed it is and from what animal) and microbial flora of the milk used, on the flora in the pinch from the previous batch transferred to the new one, and in the rennet, as well as on the microbial ecology of containers and instruments. In addition to the microbiome, variation in each step of the production process makes for a variety of different outcomes: for example, whether the milk is heated and, if so, for how long and to what temperature; the process for cooling the milk afterward and the speed at which it cools down; as well as the implements used for straining the skyr and how much it was strained. Before the age of inexpensive thermometers and reliable timepieces, women determined the temperature and time intervals using their thermal and temporal senses, trained by working in the dairy alongside other women and cultivated through years of experience, but subject of course to variation between different women and different households – traditional knowledge, in other words.

2.2 Setting Standards

Nevertheless, there were certain standards of quality, themselves traditional, against which all the diverse batches of skyr were measured: skyr that coagulated while the milk was too warm was considered too coarse and grainy and known as "stallion skyr" ("graðhestaskyr"); if the milk was too cold when the skyr coagulated, it was considered too thin and runny and known as "cold skyr" ("kaldaskyr"); and if the skyr was too sour, it was known as a "screamer" ("gellir") or at it its worst as a "devil's screamer" ("skollagellir"). And as skyr was conserved into the autumn months, it became increasingly sour. While conservation thus changed the flavor, everyone appreciated having plenty of skyr to eat out of season. On the other hand, tolerance for badly made skyr was limited and criticism forthcoming. Thus, while always recognizable as skyr, its qualities, taste, and texture varied widely between households, between regions, and over time. The microbial cultures themselves have certainly evolved over the course of the millennium plus of skyr making in Iceland. The craft of skyr making seems not have developed very much, however, until the twentieth century (Gísladóttir, 1999; Pétursdóttir, 1960, p. 15; Valsdóttir and Sveinsson, 2011) (Figure 7).

Figure 7 A woman skimming milk to make traditional skyr at home. The photo was taken in Skaftafell in the South-East of Iceland for a film project in the years 1952–1958, which aimed to preserve traditional knowledge deemed to be disappearing. Photograph by Vigfús Sigurgeirsson. Courtesy of the District Archives of Rangárvellir and Vestur-Skaftafell.

In the 1920s, the first Icelandic dairy farmers' cooperatives were created in response to a growing domestic market in urban areas. The number of milk producers had been on the rise from the beginning of the twentieth century (Gröndal, 1985, p. 7–10; Samantekt um langa sögu mjólkurafurða og starfssögu Mjólkurbús Flóamanna, 1973, p. 10–11) (Figure 8). Nevertheless, the development of the dairy industry faced various obstacles: inefficiency, competition between farms (many of which sold directly to bakeries and other food producers), as well as uneven hygiene in the small units of production and the chain of distribution. Concerns about diminishing revenues for dairy farmers' cooperatives prompted the Icelandic government in 1934 to pass legislation to regulate milk production and distribution. The law gave the various regional dairy farmers' cooperatives a monopoly license on milk distribution, which consolidated the role of dairy stores in more densely populated areas from which consumers had to buy milk and all other dairy products. Although the issue was both political and economic, one of the principal arguments revolved around hygiene standards and the need to pasteurize milk centrally before

Figure 8 The dairy of the farmers cooperative in Selfoss in the south of Iceland, newly built in 1931. Photographer unknown. Courtesy of the National Museum of Iceland.

selling to consumers, a topic hotly debated in parliament before a majority voted to require it by law (Einarsson, 1965, p. 25–70; Gröndal, 1985, p. 18–19; Guðmundsson, 2005, p. 24–34).

These were the early days of industrial production of skyr but gradually it transformed the process and the products. Responsible for this modernizing process was a new profession: dairy scientists. As the industrial and technological know-how was limited in Iceland at that time, Danish dairy scientists had to be imported to the country (which had just obtained political sovereignty from Denmark in 1918) (Guðmundsson, 2005, p. 19–20). Science was still a foreign agent and the Danish dairy scientists, who were all male, did not themselves have the traditional know-how to make skyr. To compensate, Icelandic women were asked to teach Danish dairy scientists basic skyr-making skills. The Danes were soon replaced by Icelandic dairy scientists, all of them educated in Copenhagen and all of them men.

The logic of mass production quickly favored cow's milk over that of sheep and goats as cows are easier to confine – thanks to their docile disposition – and give far higher milk yield per animal. In the same period, lamb meat acquired greater market value; as a result, the practice of weaning was abandoned, and lambs were allowed to feed on ewe's milk until they were slaughtered in fall (Júlíusson, 2013, p. 130–131). Hence the dairies only produced skyr from cow's milk, quickly replacing sheep skyr as the dominant variety and eventually doing away with it altogether as industrial production replaced production at home.

Figure 9 Farmers present at the general meeting of the dairy farmers' cooperative in 1961. Photograph by Jóhann Þór Sigurbergsson. Courtesy of the District Archives of Árnessýsla.

Other than that, skyr making at the dairies initially closely resembled the traditional mode of production on Icelandic farms through previous centuries, only the scale was larger. Little by little, however, the dairy scientists broke away from tradition and skyr making began to change (Figure 9).

2.3 Skill and Subordination

There is another way to tell this story. One that refers not just to hygiene, industry, economy, and science in a narrative of progress and productivity. That narrative obscures an essential part of the story: the gender of its protagonists. After all, milking was women's work and the dairy a traditional domain of female authority and skilled labor (Guðmundsson, 2024). An account from the turn of the twentieth century tells of a mayor in a rural municipality who cried from shame when his son milked the cows for his wife who was pregnant with their twelfth child (Sigurðardóttir, 1985, p. 248). Another vignette from the same period: a small farmer with one cow tries desperately to replace the woman who had worked for him. After several failed attempts he informs a neighboring farmer with heavy heart that he now must slaughter the cow since no woman can be found (Guðmundsson, 2005, p. 19). In a book-length treatment of the history of women's work in Iceland, Anna Sigurðardóttir remarks that it was not until well into the twentieth century that men in

Figure 10 Dairy scientists and workers at the dairy farmers cooperative in Selfoss in the 1930s. Photographer unknown. Courtesy of Akureyri Museum.

Iceland no longer found it disgraceful to milk a cow. With a note of sarcasm, she adds that soon thereafter milking machines were introduced to all larger farms (Sigurðardóttir, 1985, p. 248) (Figure 10).

Prior to the twentieth century, the dairy was often at a remote location by the summer pastures, sometimes at considerable distance from the farm. The dairy was populated exclusively by women except for one shepherd, usually a teenage boy. Sheep, goats, and cows were milked at the dairy, where the dairywomen also filtered the milk, skimmed the milk of its cream, churned the cream, kneaded the butter, curdled the skyr, and separated the whey. It was hard work and the hours were long, from the wee hours of the morning until late at night. But it was also skilled work, requiring a great deal of know-how that belonged exclusively to women. The mistress of the farm directed the work, or a housekeeper on her behalf, and most tasks in the dairy required ingenuity, skill, and sensitivity of all the women who worked there – an ability to anticipate and infer how food would taste from "how things look, feel to the hand, smell (outside the mouth), and sound" and by tasting the "food at a distance by

Figure 11 The mistress of the farm Hof in Dýrafjörður, Guðmunda Jónsdóttir, milking a cow outside during summer around 1945. Photograph by Amatörvinnustofa G. Ásgeirssonar. Courtesy of the Reykjavík Museum of Photography.

activating the sense memories of taste and smell" (Kirshenblatt-Gimblett, 1999, p. 3) (Figure 11). Thus, to churn the butter and curdle the skyr, the milk had to be heated to a particular temperature, which the mistress or housekeeper determined with her finger; to the trained ear, the sound from the churn revealed how far churning had progressed and when the butter was ready for kneading (Sigurðardóttir, 1985, p. 250) (Figure 12).

We can learn more about such sensory knowledge and skilled labor through contemporary cases. In a fascinating ethnography of dairying, Reichhardt et al. thus note that "in the Alps, cheese makers test and taste the acidity of their starter cultures every morning," while in Mongolia, "herders constantly care for their dairy products through taste, smell, touch and listening. . . . Listening to the fizzing sound of airag and checking for the presence of bubbles dancing around on the top are two methods used to check whether the ferment is alive and healthy" (Reichhardt et al., 2021, p. S346).

As historian Deborah Valenze remarks in an article on women's work and the dairy industry in England (in the eighteenth and nineteenth centuries), the "dairy presented a world of labor unto itself, topsy-turvy in its assignments of gender roles" where "the workforce, headed by a woman, was primarily female" (Valenze, 1991, p. 158); she adds that "the qualities assigned to women and men in the dairy virtually inverted the roles of the sexes: women

Figure 12 The mistress of the farm Borg, Inga Ásgrímsdóttir, churning butter in 1944. Photograph by Guðbjörg María Benediktsdóttir. Courtesy of the Reykjavík Museum of Photography.

combined decision-making with industry, and showed ceaseless commitment to a never-ending workday, while men appeared on the scene only sporadically to contribute unskilled labour" (Valenze, 1991, p. 160). With the late arrival of industrial capitalism, the same held true for the dairy in Iceland until after the First World War (Guðmundsson, 2024).

An early phase of the rationalization of dairy work in Iceland involved the creation of creameries at the turn of the twentieth century. They collected cream from farms in their district to churn butter for sale in towns and villages; the skimmed milk was either left behind at the farms or returned to them after separation at the creamery. If the establishment of creameries marked the formal entry of butter into the market economy (and out of the feudal economy of rent extraction), skyr remained for the time being a part of subsistence farming. The creameries were directed by creamery keepers ("rjómabússtýra"), who had all received a formal five-month education in dairying, and each one employed several creamery assistants, who had trained for two and a-half months at the same institution, the Dairy School founded by the Agricultural Society of Iceland in the summer of 1900 (Ívarsson and Lýðsson 2005, p. 11–13). Nearly 200 creamery keepers and assistants graduated from the Dairy School before its dissolution in

Figure 13 The mistress of Baugsstaðir farm, Kristín Jóhannsdóttir, stands by the waterfall that was harnessed to power the Baugsstaðir creamery. Photographer unknown. Courtesy of the District Archives of Árnessýsla.

1918, all of them women (Figure 13). The creameries offered practically the only independent employment outside the home available to women at the time. These jobs were better paid than domestic work and farm labor and they were in great demand. Like the remote farm dairies, the creameries were led by women and offered positions of responsibility, requiring knowledge and skill (Ívarsson and Lýðsson, 2005, p. 13–14; Sigurðardóttir, 1985, p. 257–264) (Figure 14).

The age of the creameries did not last long, however. In the 1920s and 1930s, they were disbanded one by one, and the very last one closed in 1952 (reopening as a creamery museum in 1975 and still leads that second life, as a representation of itself, fifty years later) (Ívarsson and Lýðsson, 2005, p. 51–58). From the 1920s onward, the creameries were replaced by the new industrial dairies. Many of these were dairy farmers' cooperatives; others were privately run, including the dairy at Korpúlfsstaðir, which provided the capital of Reykjavík with most of its dairy from 1929 into the 1930s (Bernharðsson,

Figure 14 The workforce of Baugsstaðir creamery in the 1930s: Margrét Andrésdóttir, Margrét Júníusdóttir (the keeper), Ágústa Júníusdóttir, and Guðrún Andrésdóttir. Photographer unknown. Courtesy of the District Archives of Árnessýsla.

2015, p. 237–239). Whether cooperative or private, however, one feature united them: an inversion of the previous gender relations in the dairy. The managers who ran the dairies were all men and next in the pecking order of the industrial dairies were the dairy scientists, also men.

Dairywomen were subordinate and contributed what increasingly came to be viewed as unskilled labor, which was gradually replaced by machines. Similar development swept over Europe at the time, for example in Bulgaria where "housewives relinquished yogurt making to male workers in small dairies" (Stoilova, 2013, p. 73). In Nordic countries such as Sweden and Denmark, women were also displaced within the dairy industry, their skilled labor slowly taken over by men and machinery during the latter half of the nineteenth and the beginning of the twentieth century (Hansen, 2006; Sommestad, 1992 and 1995). As scientific discourses and capitalist economy infiltrated the dairy, the new industrial production of dairy "displaced women from valued positions and relegated them to a more vulnerable place in a system that purported to be value-free" (Valenze, 1991, p. 169). With the economy of scale provided by large dairies with labor-saving machinery, "authority came from above and the autonomy of women was clearly circumscribed" (Valenze, 1991, p. 166). The result was the same in twentieth-century Iceland as Deborah Valenze describes a century earlier in England: "Machinery gradually performed much of the [dairy]maid's actual

Figure 15 A part of the machinery room at the dairy farmers' cooperative in Selfoss in 1930. The industrialization of dairy production played a part in the modernization of Icelandic society. Photograph by Magnús Ólafsson. Courtesy of the Reykjavík Museum of Photography.

work, while leaving a less skilled person in charge of supervising each task. At the bottom of the hierarchy, the ordinary dairymaid became part of the proletariat of the agricultural workforce" (Valenze, 1991, p. 166) (Figure 15).

Prominent mid-twentieth-century women's rights advocate Hólmfríður Pétursdóttir sums this displacement up in a coda to her own detailed description and history of traditional skyr making, published in the magazine for women's rights in 1960:

> Icelandic skyr making is a heritage from past generations of Icelandic women, women who through ingenuity, rational observation and diligence made skyr into the quality food it has been, thus contributing to maintaining the fitness and resilience of the Icelandic race in past centuries. Now Icelandic women have handed this heritage forward. It would be more correct to say, however, that economic and social transformations have seized it from them. Hopefully the nation will have the good fortune to keep preserving it for centuries yet to come. (Pétursdóttir, 1960, p. 17)

2.4 New Skyr: A Matter of Time

As the dairy industry gained momentum from the 1920s onward, home production of skyr declined. Home production of dairy food such as skyr and butter was time consuming and the depopulation of rural areas after the turn of the twentieth century left less labor available for such tasks. The depopulation, however, also created a consumer base in the emerging towns. Cooperatives solved this dilemma for farmers. They could produce dairy products in more economic and efficient ways in more densely populated areas. The farmers sold their milk to the dairy cooperatives, and with the money they earned, they could buy products such as skyr back from the cooperatives. A law passed in 1934 gave full monopoly on dairy distribution to such local farmers' cooperatives and outlawed private dairy companies. New production methods and declining home production of skyr also meant that differences in taste and texture, between farms and regions, diminished steadily in the twentieth century.

The dairy scientists at the industrial dairies – as agents of modernity – had three principal concerns: scale, time, and standard. Modernizing the making of skyr meant rendering the production process more efficient to produce greater quantities in less time but also to extend the product's shelf life. The most time-consuming aspect of making skyr was the straining (Figure 16). Many of the technological innovations throughout the century aimed to scale up and accelerate

Figure 16 Straining skyr in the industrial dairy prior to the advent of microfiltration technology. Photographer unknown. Courtesy of MS Icelandic Dairies.

the process of producing more skyr in less time. In 1942, one of the largest dairy farmer's cooperatives (Mjólkurbú Flóamanna) introduced a new centrifugal straining technology to replace the various cloth-straining frames; this sped up the straining process by a whole day and freed up time previously spent on cleaning the frames (Samantekt um langa sögu mjólkurafurða og starfssögu Mjólkurbús Flóamanna, 1973, p. 10–11). A further step in this same direction was taken in 1965–1968, when two of the biggest dairy cooperatives (MS Dairies and Mjólkurbú Flóamanna) experimented with the use of a new mechanical centrifuge to separate the whey from the curd, which was even more cost and time effective but also made the texture of the finished product softer and more uniform. In 1968, moreover, the cooperatives began to pasteurize skyr, to select the bacteria and yeast that went into it and manage microbial variation. This innovation meant that skyr could last five to seven days in a refrigerator before it gradually turned sourer to the tongue due to the ongoing fermentation in the "finished" product. The product became known at the time as "the new skyr" and was a subject of some controversy (Nýjung í skyrgerð og skyrsölu, 1968).

Moreover, the innovations sought to standardize the production process, creating in each batch of skyr a product that resembled the last batch, minimizing variations in texture and taste. For that purpose, it proved necessary to standardize both the milk and the live microbial cultures used to make skyr. Much of the research conducted by the Icelandic dairy scientists who followed the Danish ones served this purpose (Guðmundsson and Kristbergsson, 2016). Successive innovations have progressively eliminated the fungi from the skyr microbiome in an attempt to simplify, standardize, and extend shelf life. In addition to multiple strains of *Streptococcus thermophilus* and *Lactobacillus* bacteria, traditional skyr contained numerous fungal species of yeasts and molds; together, these microbes formed stable and resilient symbiotic communities that bred anew in each batch of skyr. Already in the 1910s, microbiologist Gísli Guðmundsson successfully isolated clear skyr cultures (without fungal species) with the purpose of stabilizing the fermentation process and creating a more standard product with longer shelf life; the motivation for these experiments was to create skyr that could be exported. As a sidenote, it is remarkable that the idea of exporting skyr is more than a century old, coinciding with the diffusion of Bulgarian yogurt. Nonetheless, Guðmundsson was forthcoming about his opinion that this "clear skyr" did not taste as good as traditional skyr with symbiotic microbiomes containing bacteria and fungi: "I believe this is because common skyr always contains yeast, which contributes a little bit of alcohol to the skyr as well as various unstable chemical compounds that undoubtedly improve its taste" (Guðmundsson, 1914, p. 10). He adds, however, that in this traditional fermentation of skyr, the yeast create a favorable environment for bacteria that will eventually turn the alcohol into vinegar, destroying the pleasant taste over time (Guðmundsson, 1914, p. 10–11).

In 1956 scientists at Mjólkurbú Flóamanna succeeded for the first time in producing skyr from skimmed milk powder, an innovation that made it possible to produce skyr year-round; up until then, there had been a skyr shortage in winters. The new skyr-making process pioneered by MS Dairies and Mjólkurbú Flóamanna in 1968 made this a standard procedure, replacing fresh skimmed milk with skimmed milk powder also in summer, thus eliminating seasonal variation in the principal ingredient (Samantekt um langa sögu mjólkurafurða og starfssögu Mjólkurbús Flóamanna, 1973, p. 10–11).

Another major innovation in 1968 involved the packaging of "the new skyr" in 500-gram plastic containers as prepackaged consumer goods (milk only began to be sold in cartons three years earlier) (Samantekt um langa sögu mjólkurafurða og starfssögu Mjólkurbús Flóamanna, 1973, p. 10–11). Up until this point, skyr had been sold over the counter by weight (and milk by volume) in the dairy monopoly stores, scooped up from a barrel, cut into slices, and packed in parchment (to be stirred up at home with milk, cream, or whey as well as sugar). With deregulation of dairy distribution in the 1970s, both the barrels and the new plastic containers moved into grocery stores. Plastic eventually prevailed; the last skyr was scooped up into brown paper and weighed on a grocery store scale sometime in the 1980s. Among other effects, prepackaging skyr under sterilized conditions in the dairy eliminated the introduction of environmental microbiome at the point of retail, further regimenting the product's microflora and standardizing its taste.

Vísir, one of Iceland's principal newspapers at the time, dedicated its "Women's Page" on February 28, 1969, to skyr debates, interviewing four specialists, all men, about the merits of the "new skyr" – a bacteriologist, a dairy manager, a veterinarian, and a public food safety supervisor:

> "The new skyr" as the skyr in the plastic containers is usually called has been much discussed recently, or since it was launched onto the market. It has been criticized a great deal, sometimes without due cause but sometimes for good reasons. We have now sought information from four men well-versed in these matters and asked them to respond to a few questions about the new skyr, ... its proportion of dry matter and bacterial contents, the methods of production, and the health benefits. We also asked whether they considered it plausible that it entailed the extinction of the Icelandic art of skyr making as it has been practiced here through the centuries. (Nýja skyrið, 1969, p. 5)

The bacteriologist Sigurður Pétursson responded that the bacterial flora still had quite a bit of variation and that the methods of production were more convenient and far more hygienic but "no less Icelandic." As for the health benefits: "As long as part of the skyr bacteria stay alive, I believe this skyr is just as healthy as the old one." The manager of the Mjólkurbú Flóamanna dairy cooperative Grétar Símonarson noted that the bacterial content was "certainly very different and far smaller," adding, however, that the new skyr was "in most regards produced in the same way as the old skyr" apart from the final phase of production where the method of straining differed as well as the heating, which was identical to the process used for producing "yogurt." Yogurt is enclosed in quotation marks in the article as it had not yet been introduced to the Icelandic market, but dairy scientists at Mjólkurbú Flóamanna were already experimenting with its production at the time of the interview and launched its yogurt three years later, in 1972 (in plastic containers). That same year, the dairy cooperative also launched prepackaged skyr with blueberries, the first (and for long the only) flavored variety of skyr (Samantekt um langa sögu mjólkurafurða og starfssögu Mjólkurbús Flóamanna, 1973, p. 10–11).

In the interview for the "Women's Page" in 1969, the dairy cooperative's veterinarian, Guðbrandur Hlíðar, claims that the most important bacteria are in the new skyr, along with the yeast, whereas "the old skyr contains innumerable bacteria that are hard to research and account for." There is no difference between skyr made from fresh or dried skimmed milk, according to him. As for the Icelandic art of skyr making, the veterinarian points out that the bacterial composition of the new skyr was determined by an Icelandic dairy scientist, Sævar Magnússon, who had studied Icelandic skyr for his final exam project in Norway; to him this was guarantee enough for the quality of the new production method. The public food safety supervisor, Þórhallur Halldórsson, quoted last, expresses his approval of the improved hygiene involved in prepackaging at the site of production. His main concern is that the proportion of dry matter is inferior (18.6% compared to 21% in "the old skyr") as in order to fill the new plastic containers the dairy had to increase the liquid contents; in his view, this ought to be reflected in the price to consumers. The journalist for the "Women's Page" closes by noting that "as those who have tasted these two types of skyr already know, there is some difference in the taste, and people hold very different opinions as to which tastes better, which is of course a matter of taste" (Nýja skyrið, 1969).

2.5 Cultural Diversity

A matter of taste and perspective. From the microbiome perspective, the difference was vast. The long species interaction of skyr microbiome and humans, reaching back before Iceland's settlement, possibly as far back as the end of the Bronze Age, was cut short by these innovations. A mutualistic symbiotic relationship between companion species, lasting more than a millennium and based in reciprocity, was replaced by a parasitic relationship, where one organism uses the other to its own advantage and the other's detriment. The innovation of "new skyr," and the gradual abandonment of "old skyr," was nothing less than a catastrophe for the skyr microbiome, with disastrous results for variation.

New production methods and declining home production of skyr meant that differences in taste and texture between farms and regions diminished steadily throughout the twentieth century. In our youth in the 1970s and 1980s, there were still a number of dairy cooperatives, each with slightly different equipment, techniques, and microbial cultures, not to mention the different farms and cows that supplied milk. Hence, skyr was produced with subtle local differences in texture and flavor. None of it was quite like the skyr of the former centuries, and all of it had progressively been altered and adjusted through innovations in dairy science and microbiology, the rationalization of work, the industrialization of production, the regimentation of the microbiome, and the standardization of the product. However, these had not yet taken the same form everywhere. Local dairy cooperatives had already begun to merge in order to build bigger and more efficient regional units, further advancing standardization and reducing variation. This process of mergers and acquisitions gathered momentum in the 1990s and into the early 2000s. By the turn of the century, only two remained, Auðhumla in the north and MS Dairies in the south of Iceland. In 2006–2007, they too merged under the label MS Iceland Dairies, which has since had an effective monopoly on dairy production in Iceland (Saga Auðhumlu, 2025; Um fyrirtækið, 2025). Alongside the restructuring of the industrial dairy sector, fundamental changes were made to the production and distribution of skyr. In 2001, MS Iceland Dairies launched a new brand of skyr on the domestic market, marketed as "a new generation of skyr." Named "Skyr.is," it became the flagship in Iceland's skyr production, sidelining other varieties or pushing them off the market (Figure 17).

It was a deliberately modern brand at the cutting edge of innovation, signaled through its name (Ný kynslóð af skyri, 2001, p. 9). This was during the heyday of the dot.com economy, and adding the country domain extension ".is" was meant to convey its adaptation to the lifestyles of a new generation of health-conscious millennials on the go. In the new streamlined production process for Skyr.is, an ultrafiltration process replaced centrifugal straining for separating the curds from the whey. This was partly a matter of efficiency, for ultrafiltration cuts the time needed for separation nearly in half so that it is done within a day. An added benefit, from the point of view of food technology and nutrition science, is that this process left part of the whey proteins in the skyr instead of

Figure 17 Skyr.is, a new generation of skyr launched in 2001 to feed the millennials. Photographer unknown. Courtesy of MS Icelandic Dairies.

extracting them through the filtration process. Higher protein levels create an even smoother, creamier texture in the final product.

Skyr.is was marketed in single-serving containers of 170 grams with a plastic spoon attached to the lid, rather than the standard 500-gram family container. It came in four different flavors, none with the old, familiar, sour taste of skyr. While sweet-flavored skyr had been marketed prior to this time, the varieties had, up until this point, been limited to adding blueberries or strawberries to the skyr prior to packaging, building on an older tradition of preserving berries in skyr. And more flavors soon followed, all with added sugar or artificial sweeteners. At the beginning of the millennium, MS Dairies thus succeeded in creating an even higher-protein, low-fat, velvety, sweet-flavored skyr marketed in single servings to protein-craving, fat-averse, health-conscious, sweet-toothed millennials in need of a quick fix during a meeting at the startup.

The most important difference from the microbial perspective, however, had neither to do with packaging nor protein, no more than texture or taste. In producing Skyr.is, the food engineers at MS Iceland Dairies took a final step toward the full standardization of the skyr production process by eliminating entirely the transmission of live microbial cultures from one batch of skyr to the next. The traditional method of using a pinch of old skyr to produce new skyr was now dropped in preference for ready-made, single-use packages of purchased freeze-dried bacterial cultures produced in an industrial chemical laboratory setting.

In an ethnography of traditional cheese making in the Italian Alps, anthropologist Cristina Grasseni refers to such replacement of natural or empirical starter cultures with industrial or cultivated ferments as "reterritorialization."

First, "the contingent processes of milk contamination from contact with the environment to processing tools, to maturing departments, is erased whilst milk itself is sterilized before processing, a de facto "deterritorialization" of the milk. "Reterritorialization (on the microscopic scale) comes in the shape of cultivated ferments being inserted in the curd." Adding freeze-dried cultures is a standardizing step, as Grasseni explains: "Cultivated ferments guarantee the consistency which customers supposedly ask for, but greatly reduce the scope for local variation" (Grasseni, 2011, p. 11). In the case at hand, we observe a shift from the local to the national; while erasing local variation, MS Iceland Dairies highlight the national distinction of Icelandic skyr; deterritorialization of the microbiome of the farm, animal, and instruments followed by reterritorialization with standardized "Icelandic" skyr cultures: a nationalization of skyr.

The logic guiding standardization in this case is not least that of risk management as production has been scaled up, as a product developer at MS Iceland Dairies, Björn Sigurður Gunnarsson, explained in our interview: "There is too much at stake, too much risk with all the amount of milk used" to leave skyr making to the caprice of live mother cultures from the last batch of skyr. Instead, MS Iceland Dairies relies on freeze-dried cultures from selected strains that are cloned (and hence always identical) abroad by Danish-based bioscience company, Chr. Hansen, a global supplier of food cultures, probiotics, and enzymes. This, of course, is a fundamental break with tradition, but entirely in keeping with contemporary practice in commercial dairy production, which prefers isolated bacterial strains, whereas traditional heirloom cultures are complex communities of bacteria and yeasts that have evolved together and have a structure to them that guarantees their resilience and consistency even as they allow for variation and evolution over time (Gatti et al., 2014; Kasper, 2013; Rest, 2021). With this latest innovation, skyr finally became an entirely standardized dairy product, one that always tastes, smells, looks, and feels the same.

Recent results on the microbial diversity in skyr confirm this change. Unpublished research from microbiologists and food scientists at Matís ohf (Icelandic Food Research Organization) on cultivated microbial communities from skyr is unequivocal in this regard. Samples were taken from three different sources: two small farms in Iceland that had kept the old tradition of passing on the mother skyr culture to the next batch of skyr for an unknown number of years and from skyr produced at industrial scale. The study revealed a large difference in the microbial numbers and diversity between the farm skyr cultures and the industrial ones. The farm skyr in both cases showed much higher numbers of cells and contained similar isolated species and strains of bacteria and yeasts, while the isolates from the industrial skyr were far fewer and contained homogenic bacterial isolates of *Streptococcus thermophilus*. In contrast, both traditional farm skyr cultures contained not only *Streptococcus thermophilus* but also *Lactobacillus bulgaricus* and two yeast species, *Kluyveromyces marxianus* and *Saccharomyces cerevisiae* (cf. Valsdóttir et al., 2011). These findings are consistent with previous results from Guðmundsson (1914) and Pétursson (1939), though these older studies found even more species of yeast in their traditional skyr cultures.

Moreover, the bacterial and yeast species isolated from the skyr from both farms showed significant differences on a strain level. This diversity was observed with 16S rRNA (Marteinsson et al., 2010) and 18S rRNA (Castillo-Castillo et al., 2016) genes sequencing of the bacteria and yeast, respectively. MaldiTof Biotyper (Bruker MALDI Biotyper®) analysis based on protein mass spectrometry was also used for strain distinctions. In contrast to the diversity among the skyr strains from the two farms, *Streptococcus thermophilus* isolates from the industrial skyr were identical, as revealed by these modern molecular techniques. Further research is needed to estimate how important the role of different species and strains is in skyr making and in obtaining the characteristics of the final product.

2.6 Skyr Wars

If the "original settlers" were responsible for bringing live skyr and cultures to Iceland, it took more than a millennium for the "original cultures" to leave home (again) and set sail to foreign lands (Figure 18). At the beginning of the twenty-first century, MS Iceland Dairies began to export skyr to foreign markets, at first

Figure 18 Ísey skyr was the new brand that replaced Skyr.is. Exactly the same skyr but in new packaging. Photographer unknown.
Courtesy of MS Icelandic Dairies.

in small quantities to the Nordic countries and the United States. Around the same time, an Icelander called Sigurður Hilmarsson began to make his own skyr in New York. Sigurður (or Siggi as he would soon be known) started to experiment with skyr making in the kitchen of his flat in Tribeca in 2004. In an interview with one of Iceland's leading newspapers, Siggi recounts how much he missed Icelandic skyr when he moved to the United States to study. He found American yogurt to be way too sweet and asked his mother if she could instruct him in skyr making. Siggi's mother, however, a modern woman raised on skyr from industrial dairies, had no experience of making skyr herself. But she had a library card (another kind of mother culture) and she copied some old articles for Siggi with basic descriptions of the art of skyr making.

Starting first with a stall in the farmers' market on Union Square, in 2006, Siggi's company – The Icelandic Milk and Skyr Corporation – began to sell skyr in couple of delicacy stores in Manhattan under the brand name "Siggi's skyr" (Blöndal, 2007). MS Iceland Dairies were far from happy with Siggi's entrepreneurialism as the company had been trying for a while to gain entry to the US market and had just begun to sell MS skyr in the Whole Foods Market in New York. In response to Siggi's undertaking, MS Iceland Dairies claimed sole title to the word "skyr" and exclusive rights to market dairy products as skyr – they registered it as a trademark and filed an international trademark application with the World Intellectual Property Organization (WIPO). Only a year after Siggi had founded his small company and started to sell skyr, MS Iceland Dairies threatened legal proceedings against The Icelandic Milk and Skyr Corporation for naming its skyr "skyr." Asked about this, Siggi told the reporter that his lawyer assured him that the trademark would not stand if the case ever went to court. To trademark the word "skyr," Siggi added, would be similar to attempting to trademark "yogurt." Siggi didn't heed the cease-and-desist warning from MS Iceland Dairies and the disagreement never reached the courthouse. Siggi's skyr met with wild success. By 2008, every Whole Foods Store in the United States carried the brand and from there it expanded to other grocery stores. In 2015, Starbuck's began to stock Siggi's skyr. That year, Siggi's skyr had become the fastest growing yogurt brand in the United States. In 2018, The Icelandic Milk and Skyr Corporation was acquired by Lactalis, the world's largest dairy corporation with headquarters in France, which now markets Siggi's skyr globally, from Paris to Singapore. The estimated sale price was 300 million US$: not a bad return on the investment in a library card.

MS Iceland Dairies lost the battle, but it had certainly not conceded the war. Claiming the exclusive right to name its products "skyr" was a business strategy to forestall foreign competition in the export markets. It seems not to have been directed toward small dairy producers in Iceland, though it certainly raised some eyebrows in their midst. In her ethnography of cheesemakers, Cristina Grasseni suggests that "claiming sovereignty over cheese means first and foremost advocating the right to name it and the right to police its boundaries" (2017, p. 29). Both aspects were at stake in the trademark debate, for the claimant anchored its claim to exclusive rights in the national origins and history of these products, exclusive to Iceland for the past millennium at least.

In 2015, when multinational dairy corporation Arla added Arla skyr to its product line in the Nordic countries, MS Iceland Dairies asserted its right in the trademark. While MS Iceland Dairies may be a large monopoly in the Icelandic context, size is relative. Arla is the single largest dairy producer in Scandinavia and the UK, markets with a combined population of 94 million compared to Iceland's 385 thousand. Arla is based in Denmark; as a sidenote, it may be remarked that Iceland gained its sovereignty from Denmark only in the mid-twentieth century, a subtext not entirely irrelevant for understanding the skirmishes over skyr between these two dairy companies.

Arla did not desist and this time MS Iceland Dairies sought an injunction from courts to forbid Arla from marketing skyr to consumers. Upon review of the case, however, MS Dairies lost its Swedish trademark in 2015 (Skyr – Trademark or Noun?, 2015). Its only legal success was in Finland, where Arla was given a week to remove its skyr product from dairy shelves (Markkinaoikeus/Marknadsdomstolen, 2015). Two years later, however, a Finnish appeals court overturned that verdict too – a decision bemoaned by MS and its dairy farmers (Sigurgeirsson, 2018, p. 6.) Skyr, the appeals court argued, is not a brand but a generic type of dairy. One can therefore no more claim sole title to skyr than to butter or cream.

The verdict of the Finnish appeals court, moreover, contains an interesting twist; it refers to the marketing materials of MS Iceland Dairies itself to justify the invalidation of the trademark. The company, it noted, had engaged in extensive storytelling about the history of skyr in order to cement its place as a unique product from Iceland; according to the court, this storytelling in fact showed skyr to be a generic type of dairy, rather than a product unique to this company (Salonen, 2017).

The "Skyr Wars" were on but MS Iceland Dairies had lost another battle. Its executives needed a new strategy. Their solution was ingenious: giving up the claims to "skyr sovereignty" and instead taking advantage of the size and strength of their competitor. Recognizing that Arla's advertising budget is vastly superior to its own, if Arla was going to market skyr in Scandinavia and the United Kingdom then MS Iceland Dairies might as well take a ride on its coattails. We surmise that this is the reason that marketing materials for Arla

Skyr and Ísey Skyr – from packaging (featuring stylized glaciers) to advertisements (referring to "Iceland's secret" in both cases to name just one common feature among many) – are so similar. MS Iceland Dairies lined its skyr up behind that of Arla to "draft" (like one racecar drafting behind another) behind Arla's large and expensive advertising campaign for skyr. If Arla successfully introduced this kind of dairy to consumers, along with its name and country of origin, MS Iceland could focus its far more modest advertising budget on claiming its unique selling point: the cultural authenticity of its Icelandic skyr. The locus of that authenticity, naturally enough, is in the cultures.

2.7 Original Cultures™

In February 2016, scientists from Matís ohf, the Icelandic Food Research Organization, issued a document on letterhead with stamp and signature certifying the origin of the skyr cultures used by MS Iceland Dairies. If the latter could not stop transnational dairy corporations from marketing skyr, at least it could distinguish its own product from theirs:

> Herewith it is confirmed that Icelandic Skyr 1.0 culture by Chr. Hansen contains the heirloom Skyr strain *Streptococcus thermophilus St.Cth-52* (commercial name *Streptococcus thermophilus* islandicus™). The strain was isolated from an original Icelandic Skyr and it belongs to the strain collection of Matís Ltd. Icelandic Food and Biotech R&D.
>
> MS Iceland Dairies has been using this species to make their top selling product, Skyr, since the start of the company in the 1930's. This is a culture that has been passed on for centuries in Icelandic Skyr production, first processed at the farms, later by MS Iceland Dairies.

Note the slip in the certification from the particular isolated strain of the first paragraph, the cultivated ferment produced industrially by Chr. Hansen for MS Iceland Dairies, to the general species of the empirical cultures in the second paragraph, "passed on for centuries in Icelandic Skyr production." MS Iceland Dairies may have failed in its claims to skyr sovereignty, or the exclusive right to market skyr, but by brandishing its heirloom cultures it could at least perform a sort of ownership over the microbiome of skyr. Indeed, Jón Axel Pétursson, director of sales and marketing for MS Iceland Dairies, said as much in an interview with Icelandic media in 2015: "This is something we can claim, the skyr that we produce is the only one with the original skyr cultures. That is our mark of distinction" (Jakobsdóttir, 2015) (Figure 19).

In its marketing abroad, the skyr from MS Iceland Dairies is accordingly cast as "the only skyr that contains the original Icelandic skyr cultures from MS

Figure 19 At the skyr museum in Selfoss, one learns about skyr-making traditions and how they were kept alive by forty generations of women. Photographer unknown. Courtesy of MS Icelandic Dairies.

Iceland Dairies, and it's made according to the original Icelandic recipe." Indeed, the lid of the plastic container of Ísey Skyr that we bought at a local supermarket in the south of France tells consumers, "It's made with the original Icelandic skyr cultures, which help give our top quality skyr its delicious taste and texture." As a matter of fact, "Original Icelandic Skyr Cultures" is a registered trademark owned by MS Iceland Dairies, as is "The Original Icelandic Recipe."

In the United States, MS Dairies has partnered with an American venture capital investment firm, Polaris Founders Capital, to create Icelandic Provisions, a company that sells "Traditional Icelandic Skyr," as the label announces. Its advertising claims that the "reason nothing else tastes like Icelandic Provisions" is that it uses "Certified Icelandic Heirloom Skyr Cultures":

> These cultures have been treasured and preserved in Iceland for hundreds of years. In the same way that sourdough starters are passed down through families and shared between neighbors, the women of Iceland have passed this tradition on through generations to provide the cultures in your cup of Icelandic Provisions. The milk is heated to just the right temperature before adding our Original Skyr Cultures, which help transform that milk into Skyr – similar to the way Icelanders have for hundreds of years. (What is Skyr?, 2025)

The use of "Original Skyr Cultures" makes this "the only authentic Icelandic Skyr in the US market." As the quote above correctly suggests, the making of skyr through the centuries has fostered and relied on diverse fermentative microbiomes. However, the industrialization of skyr making in the twentieth and twenty-first centuries brought an end to this lineage of live skyr cultures as they ceased to be passed on from one generation to the next. Cloned, isolated bacterial strains replaced the breeding of microbial communities that survived and evolved through each batch of freshly made skyr. It was not until the traditional microbial communities had broken down that Slow Food deemed it necessary to define traditional skyr, placing emphasis on the method of using a pinch of old skyr to make new skyr. However, the opportunity presented by the newfound interest in traditional skyr was not lost on MS Iceland Dairies. As the company was not successful in claiming "Skyr" as its trademark, it shifted focus toward the live cultures themselves and the traditional recipe for skyr. Original and authentic "heirloom cultures" and the long tradition of skyr making became its unique selling points in competition with other global dairy companies. The branding of the microbiome is perhaps the most ingenious aspect of the marketing strategy devised by MS Iceland Dairies, which, alongside the high-protein/low-fat, ice-cool superfood narrative that lines its skyr up with that of Arla, relies to a considerable extent on heritage branding: the purity of its tradition and the genealogy of its practice.

3 Heritage Branding

> It fueled the exploits of Vikings and farmers for generations. Imagine what it could do for you!
>
> Iceland Provisions

We grew up in Iceland in the last quarter of the twentieth century eating skyr for breakfast or lunch many times a week, usually stirred into milk for a smoother consistency and with a bit of sugar on top to sweeten the naturally sour taste. It was also served for dessert, stirred in with cream, sugar, and blueberries. Skyr was the most commonplace of foods: healthy, tasty, effortless, easy to serve, easy to eat, and easy to digest. It is a simple food; it demanded neither skill nor time nor historical consciousness. Our skyr was not homemade and was not from the dairies of individual farms, where skyr making and other dairy work was historically the domain of women and required both skill and experience as we recounted in the previous section. The skyr that we grew up on was, for the most part, produced under the supervision of dairy scientists in the country's four largest dairy cooperatives, two in the southwest – in the capital city of Reykjavík and the neighboring agricultural town of Selfoss – and two in the biggest towns in the North – Akureyri and Húsavík. Crucially, we did not grow up thinking of skyr as food heritage. That was just not part of the public imagination and skyr-eating was neither a reflexive practice nor one with an explicit temporal dimension. We all ate skyr, all the time, and it never occurred to us to consider it in the context of women's culture or its microbial legacy. It is possible that we were unusually unreflexive children, but as far as we know, Icelanders of all ages ate skyr without giving much thought to all that. This was about to change at the beginning of the twenty-first century.

As a newly minted heritage food, the past years have seen skyr transformed from unremarkable everyday fare to remarkable food heritage, marketed as such at home in Iceland but even more so abroad. This transformation has assigned skyr a new position within the cultural landscape and a distinct place on the dairy shelf through an attempt to create novel associations between producer, consumer, place, and product. Such production of multiple and complex cultural contexts – or the commercialization of cultural and historical references – has come to play an ever-expanding role in alimentary customs in the contemporary world (Amilien et al., 2005; Jónsson, 2013; Köstlin, 1998; Pétursson, 2013 and 2018; Tschofen, 1998, 2008 and 2017).

The story of skyr as heritage contributes to growing scholarship on cheese-heritagemaking in Europe and North America (Grasseni, 2011, 2012 and 2017; May, 2013; Paxson, 2008, 2010, 2013 and 2014b; Petridou, 2012; Tschofen, 2008 and 2017; West, 2020). Cristina Grasseni notes that the reinvention of cheese as heritage depends on "continuous intervention, including commercial tactics, symbolic politics and the pervasive performance of a culture of discernment (gustatory, sensorial, historical, genealogical, geographic, agronomic and culinary)" (Grasseni, 2017, p. 6). This description aptly captures the transformation of skyr into heritage, as domestic and international skyr producers try to establish bonds between people, places, and products. Moreover, European ethnologist Bernhard Tschofen remarks that many European cheese varieties owe their newfound appreciation as traditional or heritage products to growing global attention to local and regional specialties (May, 2013; Tschofen, 2017, p. 120–125). Here, we focus on how the global heritage branding of skyr redefines locality and adds value to the product.

The international marketing of skyr glides effortlessly from Icelandic medieval literature to modern healthy living in an attempt to promote skyr as a unique, authentic, and wholesome product. Food producers and businesses, as well as the global tourism industry, have spotted an opportunity for profit in marketing their products with reference to temporality and spatiality, through concepts of tradition and heritage, on the one hand, and place and the local, on the other. Narratives and images are conveyed through advertisements, labeling, and packaging, setting the scene for new forms of engagement between

Figure 20 A UK skyr ad from MS Iceland Dairies celebrating generations of women. Photographer unknown. Courtesy of MS Icelandic Dairies.

producers and consumers (Figure 20). In what follows, we seek to lay bare messy relationships between local and global in such heritage efforts; the case of skyr illustrates some of the ways in which global trends and markets influence how people at local levels think about and act on their own cultural forms, and how the local level then impacts global flows.

3.1 Skyr Becomes Heritage

As a new century dawned upon the countryside, the home production of skyr had almost completely disappeared. A study conducted in 2010 found that a mere three farms out of over 3,000 in the country still produced their own skyr, still using what food scientists call "empirical starters" or "undefined starters," that is, an inoculum from the previous batch of skyr to start a new one (Valsdóttir and Sveinsson, 2011). Traditions do not come much closer to extinction than this. As of 2024, there are four farms that make traditional skyr. Not exactly exponential growth.

Sensing danger, the Slow Food Reykjavík Convivium, the local chapter of the international eco-gastronomic movement, mobilized to preserve skyr and succeeded in registering skyr on Slow Food's Ark of Taste in 2007. The Ark of Taste travels around the world, searching for small-scale, local products "that belong to the cultures, history, and traditions of the entire planet" and that members of Slow Food believe to be endangered by "industrialization, genetic erosion, changing consumption patterns, climate change," etc. The Ark's aim is to save these products from the deluge of mass production via their rediscovery, supporting producers and telling their stories in an attempt to help the food find its way back into people's kitchens and onto their dining tables (Ark of Taste).

The Reykjavík Convivium was concerned that the definition of skyr had been confused by all the changes in the production process. Its members were convinced of the economic and cultural potential of traditional skyr and believed that these possibilities ought to be highlighted through increased production, promotion, and development. As a first step, however, the Convivium deemed it urgent to safeguard traditional skyr to prevent its extinction. It is precisely this context of urgency that created the need to define what traditional skyr is.

"The traditional recipe is complex," notes the homepage of the Slow Food Foundation for Biodiversity before it provides a step-by-step description of the correct method for making traditional skyr and concludes with an enumeration of what distinguishes the traditional dairy product from its industrial counterpart (Traditional Icelandic Skyr). This traditional recipe is certainly complex, but we suggest that its complexity may have more to do with the task of definition than the actual process of making skyr. According to historical accounts, there was no specific traditional recipe; this accounts for the great variation in both its taste and texture (Gísladóttir, 1999, p. 67–68). It is only through its heritagization that a standard definition of a traditional recipe came into being. Although the Slow Food movement's goal is to safeguard and promote biological, cultural, and gastronomic diversity, Slow Food's definition of traditional skyr and of the recipe for its making actually introduces a heritage standard and a stock narrative. As we will see, industrial producers have appropriated this narrative to legitimize cultural claims in the branding and marketing of their own products.

Complex though the recipe for traditional skyr may be, it betrays a clear conception of what it is not. Slow Food emphasizes that the main differences between traditional skyr and its industrialized counterpart are, first, the use of a pinch of older skyr to make a new batch and, second, a lengthy preparation time using traditional methods for straining, that is, to separate the skyr from the whey. To make skyr the old-fashioned way is, therefore, to slow down the process, an antidote to temporal acceleration in the industrial food system.

Through this definition of traditional skyr, the microbial cultures emerge as bearers of tradition and guarantors of historical continuity. Preserving skyr to make new skyr, giving the bacteria and yeast a new lease on life in a new batch of skyr, the dairy product is anchored in past cultural traditions while slowly guiding the present towards the future. Folklorist Henry Glassie proposes to define tradition as "the creation of the future out of the past" (Glassie, 1995, p. 395). Indeed, the future is precisely the point at issue here. The following appeal appears in a beige frame below the recipe for traditional skyr: "The challenge to save biodiversity is not just any challenge. At stake is the future of the planet and the human race. Join us and do your part: support Slow Food" (Traditional Icelandic Skyr).

Subsequent to the successful listing of skyr on the Ark of Taste, Slow Food established a presidium, or local committee, around traditional skyr in 2015 with the aim of preserving the traditional recipe. The presidium emphasizes the protection and promotion of small-scale farmers and producers to help them survive within a new rural economy but "also wants to encourage the development of gastronomic tourism focused on the ancient food traditions still found around the country" (Traditional Icelandic Skyr).

Three producers belong to this presidium, Erpsstaðir Creamery in the west of Iceland, a family farm about which we have more to say below; Egilsstaðabú in the east of Iceland, a large family farm with a café, boutique, and guesthouse; and Skaftholt farm in the south of Iceland, an organic/biodynamic sustainable farm and home for people with developmental disabilities (Figure 21). With the presidium

Figure 21 Baldur Gauti Gunnarsson, farmer and shopkeeper at Egilsstaðabú making traditional skyr for the authors during their fieldwork. Photograph by Jón Þór Pétursson.

project, Slow Food acts as an intermediary between producers and consumers and tries to establish connections between different producers. The presidium promotes their products by telling the story of skyr, its makers, and the area it comes from. In adding traditional skyr to the Ark of Taste and creating a presidium to preserve and promote the product, Slow Food locates skyr within a new cultural context as heritage, a context that emphasizes difference over standardization.

3.2 Old-Fashioned Skyr

In the valley of Búðardalur, in the west of Iceland, lies Erpsstaðir Creamery. The farmers are Þorgrímur Einar Guðbjartsson and Helga Elínborg Guðmundsdóttir, both with family roots in the Dalasýsla district (Figure 22). Þorgrímur is a dairy

Figure 22 Þorgrímur Einar Guðbjartsson at Erpsstaðir Creamery fills a cloth bag with freshly made skyr before the straining begins. Photograph by Helga Elínborg Guðmundsdóttir.

scientist by education and previously worked for MS Iceland Dairies in Búðardalur in the last decade of the twentieth century. He and Helga were interested in homemade products, and in 2006 they began to expand the farm. When construction was over in 2009, the Erpsstaðir Creamery began operating, creating conditions to reduce the distance between producers and consumers, a move contrary to the centralization of dairy production over the previous one hundred years.

When expanding, the couple designed the cowshed to receive tourists and provide them with a first-hand experience of the production process. On a guided tour, visitors are led through the barn, where they can snuggle with calves while watching through a glass window as dairy robots milk the cows. From there, they stroll over to the next window displaying the making of skyr and ice cream. Finally, they can round off the experience sitting down and relaxing in the small café while enjoying the food whose production they have just witnessed.

In 2009, the farm began to produce ice cream and sell it in their farm shop. The skimming of cream for this ice cream, however, left large quantities of skimmed milk as a byproduct. To begin with, the skimmed milk was fed to the calves, but soon Helga and Þorgrímur decided to try their luck with skyr-making. Production of ice cream for tourists thus created the Erpsstaðir skyr as a byproduct for added value, a relationship much like that of butter production to skyr-making in previous centuries.

The skyr from Erpsstaðir is called *Sveitaskyr* ("Country Skyr"). Þorgrímur explains in an interview in 2018 that he uses the same methods as when he worked as a dairy scientist for MS Dairies in Búðardalur in the 1990s. The skimmed milk is heated and cooled down before adding a pinch from the previous batch of skyr. After the live cultures from the last batch have acidified the milk and it has coagulated into a semi-solid state, the skyr goes into a cloth bag and is strained overnight; the whey drips into a container below, leaving the skyr curds in the bag. To obtain his "original cultures" and start making skyr, Þorgrímur got a skyr starter by buying a tub of the brand *Óhrært skyr* (literally, Unstirred skyr), produced by MS Iceland Dairies. But things got off to a shaky start:

> When I began in 2009–2010 to make my own skyr, I didn't succeed in making it coagulate. After several failed attempts, I discovered that MS Iceland Dairies had started to pasteurize its skyr, something that was not done when I worked there. The reason they started to pasteurize the skyr was to make it last longer. Instead of two-week shelf life, like it used to have, it lasts four weeks. As a result, you don't have these live cultures in the product anymore.

There simply aren't sufficient live cultures, or sufficiently live cultures, in MS skyr to breed and survive in a new batch. Unstirred Skyr is a specialty item produced without flavorings irregularly and in modest quantities by MS Iceland

Dairies in an industrial dairy in the north of the country with late twentieth century production methods – with a pinch of skyr from the previous batch. Þorgrímur still resorts to it on occasion, especially in winter. When demand drops, Þorgrímur makes less skyr, and its microbiome doesn't always survive from one batch to the next. On such occasions, Þorgrímur grabs a tub of *Óhrært skyr* in the nearest supermarket and starts the process over.

The MS Iceland Dairies monopoly produces skyr in forty-nine product variants of different flavors and sizes, marketed under three brands: *Ísey skyr*, *KEA skyr*, and *Óhrært skyr*. *Ísey Skyr* is by far the largest of these and *Óhrært skyr* is the smallest. Björn Sigurður Gunnarsson, the product developer at MS Iceland Dairies, referred in our interview to this production "in the old way" with "mother cultures" as risky business:

> We still make that sort of skyr, but . . . it could never be an export. There is too much at stake, too much risk with all the amount of milk used. But we do safeguard these old production methods and traditions with the old centrifuges and all that. But *Óhrært skyr* is not sold abroad. Its shelf life is very short; it is only a fortnight. It is a product that has a difficult time, but it is nice to have it on the domestic market, so we have kept it.

It is "nice to have" old-fashioned skyr in small quantities on a domestic retail market, where the two-week shelf life doesn't pose a serious problem, stocked as a heritage alternative next to the mainstream product on the dairy shelf in the supermarket refrigerator. Indeed, when Björn began working for MS Iceland Dairies, he was appointed to serve on the company's heritage board. Among other things, this heritage board curates a small museum and archive at the company's headquarters in Reykjavík that documents and represents the company's history, beginning with its predecessors in the creameries that antedated the various local dairy cooperatives at the beginning of the twentieth century. Besides producing dairy products, MS Iceland Dairies thus also produces the cultural and historical context for their production.

The live cultures in *Óhrært skyr*, also produced by MS, provide part of that context. Within MS Iceland Dairies, a conscious decision has thus been made to safeguard older production methods in a small dairy in the north of the country as a form of heritage that exists in parallel to the modern production. "Old-fashioned" skyr is "nice to have," as Björn puts it; it exists in the present, but it is not of the present. It has become a market niche with interesting prospects. Indeed, Björn's erstwhile boss, Einar Sigurðsson, managing director of MS from 2009 to 2015, noted in a public radio interview in 2013 that there was great interest in further developing old-fashioned skyr as a product, "especially with the tourism sector in mind" (Skyrið verður áfram íslenskt, 2013) (Figure 23).

Figure 23 MS Iceland Dairies skyr ad with the caption "Enjoy the moment". Photographer unknown. Courtesy of MS Icelandic Dairies.

3.3 Tourism and Local Food

MS Dairies thus relates potential product development of old-fashioned skyr to the expansion of tourism, an export sector industry that does not depend on shelf life. Instead of exporting products, consumers are imported. Expansion is not a term that does justice to the growth rate of tourism in Iceland. The number of foreign visitors in 2024 was 2.3 million, five times as great as it was in 2010 when there were 488,000 (Ferðamálastofa, 2024). For a population of approximately 393,000, that is a radical change. All of those visitors have to eat while in the country. Among other things, this has expanded the market for skyr with new consumers who take a different sort of interest in the product, to whom it represents local flavor and a way of experiencing local culture by tasting and ingesting it. Under these changing market conditions, the production of skyr's cultural and historical context has taken on new urgency.

Some fifty kilometers from the capital city, the small town of Selfoss played a central role in the twentieth-century history of the dairy industry and today houses most of the production of MS Iceland Dairies. Its "new old" town center, created by private developer Sigtún, is an urban development project with 53 new buildings on a large, central lot, each with the reconstructed facade of a historic building from somewhere in Iceland that, at some point, was destroyed by fire or fell into disrepair (Jónsdóttir, 2018 and 2019). Its centerpiece is a reconstruction of the old Selfoss dairy of 1929, a building designed by Iceland's most famous architect, Guðjón Samúelsson, but torn down to make way for a bigger industrial dairy building in the 1950s.

The reconstructed dairy houses a food court, events, and, above all, a skyr museum – *Skyrland* – which "takes you to the heart of Icelandic history, culture and nature, and tells you what lies behind every spoonful of skyr" (Skyrland, 2025). The importance of the skyr museum is not to be underestimated as stated on Sigtún's project website:

> We have great confidence in an exhibition on Icelandic skyr and we believe it will attract a number of visitors every year. There is a vast variety of museums and exhibitions around the world that display food culture in diverse ways. There are milk museums, beer museums, wine museums, and so forth. A skyr museum will be the first of its kind. (Miðbær Selfoss, undated)

Under the rubric "Icelandic Dairy Tale," Skyrland's homepage promises to immerse "your senses in the world of skyr, Iceland's unique superfood"; in "journey of sights, scents and tastes, you'll discover a 1000-year story of how a Viking dairy product became a global modern health food." "Skyr, the creamy Icelandic yogurt," it explains, "is woven through the story of a nation" (Skyrland, 2025).

While the museum was still in the planning stages, Ari Edwald, managing director of MS Iceland Dairies, explained in an interview the company's intention to "create some kind of domicile for skyr in Iceland as an anchor in our export of knowledge to the international market." It is a part of "the long-term marketing strategy based on a well-defined brand." That's where Skyrland fits in, to strengthen the storytelling behind the brand, as Edwald spelled out:

> We are currently in 15 countries. We have made it our goal to be in 22 countries in four or five years. But I suspect things will go even faster than that. In fact, all the countries in the world may be involved. It is in this context that we are interested in creating an international home for Icelandic skyr in Selfoss. (Endurreisn Gamla mjólkurbúsins liður í markaðsstarfi MS 2018)

There is an interesting logic that the managing director makes explicit; the localization of skyr is a part of the international marketing strategy. The export of skyr, in other words, creates its local identity as a byproduct. The branding of skyr as particularly Icelandic began with the surge in tourism but continues with the marketing of MS skyr for consumers around the world. Building a distinct brand identity from competitors on the international dairy market, skyr's localization adds value to the product. A part of this brand construction is

Figure 24 The Skyrland exhibition in Selfoss recounts the story of skyr making in Iceland from the time of settlement until the present day. Photographer unknown. Courtesy of MS Icelandic Dairies.

a furbishing of history and a "symbolic recalibration" (Grasseni, 2017, p. 8) of skyr as a national heritage food (Figure 24).

3.4 Skyr Heritage: Theaters of Authenticity

In the neighboring town of Hveragerði, not even ten miles from the "new old" dairy in Selfoss, stands a building erected as the country's first skyr processing plant. Designed for the local dairy cooperative by the same renowned architect as the Selfoss dairy, *Skyrgerðin* ("The Skyr Factory") opened in 1930, but has been home to various restaurants that have come and gone since the 1950s. In 2016, a new owner refurbished it as a restaurant and guesthouse, reinstating the old name *Skyrgerðin*. The history of the house was set front and center since the owner installed old-fashioned skyr-making equipment in the middle of the building, where the restaurant made cloth-strained skyr. "We are going to show our guests how skyr is made and give them a taste of it, so we offer historical and gastronomic tourism," explained the owner, entrepreneur Elfa Dögg Þórðardóttir. She added that "we have an elegant guesthouse, a beautiful bistro, and finally skyr production again, which is nice since skyr is making it big all over the world" (Skyrgerðin opnuð í Hveragerði, 2017).

Visitors to the Skyr Factory were offered a thirty-minute guided tour to learn about "the full history of skyr making from our master skyr maker, taste different types of skyr, and see some of the old equipment that was used to make skyr in the past." Appropriately enough, the master skyr maker in the Skyr Factory was actor and chef Erlendur Eiríksson, who has over a dozen IMDB credits to his name. As the owner put it, "[y]ou might say we take full advantage of his strengths because a visit to the Skyr Factory should be an experience for the mind, the hand, and the taste buds at the same time" (Skyrgerðin í Hveragerði færir út kvíarnar, 2017). Alas, the Skyr Factory fell victim to the Covid Pandemic; as a result, Eiríksson turned from dairy to plants and is now a master cheesemaker at *Livefood*, a geothermal vegan cheese producer in Hveragerði.

Referring to the reinvention of cheese in the Italian Alps, Cristina Grasseni notes that "the notion of tradition mobilizes a veritable theatre of authenticity whose audience anticipates and participates in the performance" (Grasseni, 2017, p. 3). In the towns of Selfoss and Hveragerði, this theatre has constructed old dairies as its stage. The traditional tools and artisanal techniques of skyr-making are interpreted with elaborate stage and museum technologies, crowned by the tasting experience, a "gastronomic ethnography" (Kirshenblatt-Gimblett, 2006, p. 5) of skyr.

Sliding a step down the food supply chain, from restaurant to farm, we find farmers who have adopted another approach to staging the authenticity of the skyr they offer for consumption. From the reconstructed industrial dairy façade in Selfoss and the refurbished skyr factory in Hveragerði, we move into the barn itself. Another fifty kilometers inland, and only fifteen minutes from Iceland's most popular destination of the Geysir hot springs area, in 2013 the siblings who own the dairy farm in Efstidalur added a guesthouse, horse rental, a restaurant in the hayloft, and an ice cream barn to their parents' farm. The ice cream production is ambitious, offering guests fresh-made Italian-style gelato with an assortment of flavors, all from cows that one can admire and pat while eating ice cream made from the milk of their udders. Much as in the case of Erpsstaðir above, the ice cream production in Efstidalur leaves a great deal of skimmed milk as a byproduct from which the farmers make skyr. Their skyr can be bought to take home in old-fashioned parchment packages and is served as a starter or dessert in the hayloft restaurant, literally overlooking the cows in the barn: "Look through the windows and enjoy a view into our stable while tasting your ice cream. It doesn't get any more farmish than this!" (Efstidalur II, 2025). One wall in the restaurant consists entirely of windows into the barn, a fourth wall in a theatre of authenticity that both curious diners and curious cows break with their mutual gaze (Figure 25).

Figure 25 Promotional photo from Efstidalur farm playfully picturing the interspecies relations so prominent in the branding of skyr. Photograph by Graatje Weber. Courtesy of Efstidalur II ehf.

As a site of culinary tourism (Long, 1998 and 2004), the Efstidalur ice cream barn and hayloft restaurant is a site of contact and encounter that is produced through "a collaboration between highly self-conscious producers and consumers" (Kirshenblatt-Gimblett, 2004, p. xi–xii) around an experience in which the farm becomes an exhibit in and of itself, cows, farmers and all. "Watch the cows while enjoying your homemade ice cream" (Efstidalur II, 2025). As you take your leisure and lick your cone, you can watch the farmers at work, farming and making ice-cream, cheese and skyr. A startling juxtaposition, this staged production of the full food supply chain is an example of what, following Barbara Kirshenblatt-Gimblett, "might be called the tourist surreal" (1998, p. 152).

All that is missing is a skyr festival. Indeed, the festival is a conventional genre of display in the field of heritage and new festivals have cropped up in recent years wherever sites and practices have been designated as cultural heritage (Hafstein, 2018). This is also the case for food heritage (such as the "festival de la frite" celebrating fries in Belgium, the "Fête du Pain" celebrating the baguette in France, and the Nsima festival, celebrating thick porridge in Malawi). It holds true, too, for traditional dairy. Thus, the village of Momchilovtsi in the Bulgarian Rhodope Mountains is well known among Chinese consumers. The Chinese dairy company *Bright Dairy & Food* has been buying and using yogurt cultures from that village since 2008. It brands its yogurt with the village name and advertises it as "authentically Bulgarian," promoting its "Momchilovtsi yogurt" as a healthy product based in ancient Bulgarian traditions of healthiness and longevity. As of 2015, "Rhodope's Traditions," a festival of yogurt in Momchilovtsi, has fanned the flames of the love affair of Chinese consumers with Bulgarian villagers. As Nevena Nancheva (2019) documents in her ethnographic account of the festival, the program includes folk dance and song, a beauty contest, a children's drawing competition, as well as the tasting and rating of home-made yogurts. Sponsored by *Bright Dairy & Food*, this is an exemplar of heritage branding, anchoring export in a local festival (rather than a local museum, as in Selfoss) and importing foreign consumers to bear witness to the source of authenticity. In fact, Chinese tourists have flooded Momchilovtsi, even prompting local villagers to start studying Mandarin (Nancheva, 2019). Perhaps MS Iceland Dairies' brand monitoring department will read this and launch an annual Festival of Skyr.

3.5 Senior Citizens in the "Skyr Lounge"

Much as in Skyrland, visitors can learn about traditional skyr-making at the Efstidalur farm, as the siblings who own it offer guided tours of the dairy where one may observe skyr in the making. The same holds true for the Erpsstaðir Creamery in the west of Iceland, where Þorgrímur and Helga began with a similar concept in 2009. In 2017, Erpsstaðir also became an ÉCONOMUSÉE®, joining a network of artisans and crafts enterprises in Canada and northern Europe. The network is designed to help the participating fine-crafts and agri-food enterprises develop their businesses and become more competitive as they reach out to the public by "transmitting their knowledge and know-how during artisan-visitor interaction," define and explain local culture and contribute to the preservation of tangible as well as intangible cultural heritage (Artisans at Work, 2025). As Þorgrímur explained, as part of becoming an ÉCONOMUSÉE®um, Erpsstaðir inaugurated a lounge to interpret skyr for visitors:

> We wound up with this skyr lounge where people can come and learn about skyr. We have some text on the walls. We have sketches, and we have 3D sculptures in addition to skyr tasting and a guided skyr tour – that's what we call it – where we recount the history of skyr, explain how it has been made through time, and I also philosophize on my theory of the origins of skyr. People who come here are fascinated to discover, really, how we managed to conserve the skimmed milk here in Iceland. Once the cream was removed and kneaded into butter for the rich folk, we could use the protein, eat it, and have the whey to preserve our food that we didn't want to spoil during winter.

The creamery has been very successful. It was well received when it opened in 2009, with approximately 5,000 visitors in the first year, a number that more than tripled in five years to some 17,000 in 2014 and stood at roughly 30,000 in 2024. Sales in skyr and ice cream have multiplied by the same factors. With both native and foreign guests, Þorgrímur distinguished between four categories of customers who appreciate his traditional skyr: the foreigners, the "protein dudes," the dieters, and the seniors.

> Senior citizens are young again when they get their good old skyr. The protein dudes come and buy a few buckets of skyr and colostrum. Then it's all those who are dieting. They like to buy skyr and here you have clean skyr without flavorings. Thanks to its consistency, it is excellent for smoothies.

When asked further about the rejuvenation of seniors, Þorgrímur explained that what they like most about his skyr is the sour taste. "There is no sugar in it, so you really feel the acidity. When I get a group of senior citizens, I just go and get a pitcher of whey and put it out. I usually need to fetch two to three pitchers. It keeps them going until they come back again."

Drawing on the work of Kirshenblatt-Gimblett, the "capacity of food to hold time, place, and memory is valued all the more in an era of hypermobility, when it can seem like everything is available everywhere all the time" (Kirshenblatt-Gimblett, 2004, p. xiii). Food experiences form "edible chronotopes" that transport people through space and time (Kirshenblatt-Gimblett, 2004, p. xiii) through a convergence of senses, emotions, and memories. As a matter of neurological fact, the insular cortex of the brain, also known as the gustatory cortex, and the olfactory bulb are closely connected to the amygdala, which is involved in emotional learning, and the hippocampus, which is central to memory. According to neuroscientists, the many connections between these areas of the brain link smell and taste closely to emotion and memory (Miranda, 2012; Shepherd, 2006; Soudry et al., 2011). Much like the smell and taste of a madeleine pastry for Marcel Proust, the taste of traditional skyr sends older people back to their youth when its acidity prickled their taste buds on a daily basis. It evokes memories, it stirs emotions; they feel young again, an emotion socially practiced and shared when tasting skyr at Erpsstaðir.

3.6 Stirring Emotions

The European Ethnologist Monique Scheer developed the concept of "emotional practices" to describe how emotion-as-practice involves "the self (as body and mind), language, material artifacts, the environment, and other people" (Scheer, 2012, p. 193). Through this definition, emotions emerge as practices embodied within a social context through bodily acts of experience and expression (Scheer, 2012 and 2016). If emotional practices are about doing emotions in everyday situations, then to taste traditional skyr is to do emotion in a way that brings a sour past to an artificially sweetened present.

In their introduction to an edited volume titled *Edible Identities*, Ronda L. Brulotte and Michael A. Di Giovine remark on the affective powers of food: "its taste on our individual tongues often incites strong emotions, while the communal, commensal experience of such sensations binds people together, not only through space but time as well, as individuals collectively remember past experiences with certain meals and imagine their ancestors having similar experiences." "When this occurs," they add, "food is transformed into heritage" (Brulotte and Di Giovine, 2016, p. 1). This transubstantiation further complicates the emotions involved in eating heritage foods, pointing beyond the autobiographical to the collective and historical.

The concept of the heritage emotions (*les émotions patrimoniales*) is derived from the work of an interdisciplinary group of researchers in France, led by ethnologist Daniel Fabre, to study popular mobilizations around threatened heritage sites (Fabre, 2013; Hottin, 2011). As the French cultural sociologist Nathalie Heinich argues, the relationship to cultural heritage is charged with emotion. "One might even say that emotion is the proof of heritage; if the proof of the pudding, as the saying goes, is in the eating, the proof of heritage would be that it moves us" (Heinich, 2012, p. 21; authors' translation). Emotions, she maintains, reveal shared values. Sharing emotions is, therefore, a way of transforming them into socially recognizable values or norms. Heritage emotions can be positively charged, as in appreciation, admiration, curiosity, attachment, and pride, or negatively charged, as in shock, anger, horror, and indignation. Either way, according to Heinich, heritage emotions relate to the value of authenticity as a connection between the present state of the object of heritage and its origins, the value of presence as a feeling of encounter or proximity to persons through the object of heritage, and aesthetic value as the beauty of the object of heritage or, indeed, of its taste. These emotions are amplified, according to Heinich, by an experience of antiquity, the presence of the past, or a relationship to ancestors, as well as by a sense of scarcity (Heinich, 2012, cf. 2009).

The theatres of authenticity on the dairy farms of Erpsstaðir and Efstidalur stage these values in encounters with artisanal farmers who "presence" the past in making skyr with traditional methods and microbial cultures made scarce through innovations in industrial dairying, documenting their antiquity in spaces of interpretation and guided skyr tours, and offering a taste of heritage to appreciative visitors from the city and from abroad. The Skyr Factory in Hveragerði replaced the dairy farmers turned actors and interpreters (in Erpsstaðir and Efstidalur) with an actor-turned-master skyr maker, and Skyrland in Selfoss goes further still in interpreting skyr heritage in an exhibition and digital installation by Snorri Freyr Hilmarsson. Snorri is a renowned theatrical set designer and film production designer, working together with the creative artists, designers, animators, programmers, producers, and film and sound specialists of Gagarín, a richly awarded multimedia company that creates interactive media solutions that allow people to experience stories vividly (Gagarín, 2025). In its own manner, each production plays on heritage emotions, designing direct experiences of the heritage values of skyr: authenticity, presence, and the aesthetics of taste. As we shall see, these forms of emotional practice carry over into the marketing of mass-produced skyr.

3.7 Adding Value

Naturally, foreign visitors to Erpsstaðir have no childhood recollections of skyr. To be sure, the sour taste of old-fashioned skyr doesn't conjure up memories and stir emotions in the same way, but nevertheless, these visitors usually have a comparison on the basis of which to judge the taste of country skyr, something that Þorgrímur himself notes:

> Like the people who came today. They already knew we make old-fashioned skyr. They came here to taste it, and they had tasted the usual store-bought skyr. They said it isn't the same product . . . No question about it. People also like tasting the whey, Icelanders and foreigners alike.

For these visitors, too, the tasting provides evidence of the transubstantiation of food into heritage and a way for them to participate directly in that heritage. As folklorist Lucy Long notes in her writings on culinary tourism, "participation occurs specifically because of the perceived otherness of the foodways," which is corroborated through the techniques of exhibition and interpretation in these skyr destinations, "and that otherness elicits curiosity." Culinary tourism, because it relies on "the senses of taste, smell, touch, and vision, offers a deeper, more integrated level of experience" than any sightseeing. Long argues that it engages "one's physical being, not simply as an observer, but as a participant as well" (Long, 2004, p. 21).

A sense of scarcity no doubt amplifies the heritage emotions of tourists who taste Þorgrímur's skyr at Erpsstaðir. They have a curiosity for and appreciation of old-fashioned country skyr, or "real skyr," a term that condenses the value of authenticity and the aesthetics of taste. The following review is from the *Reykjavík Grapevine*, an English-language magazine for foreigners in Iceland.

> You have not tried real skyr until you have had it from a real small-batch producer like Erpsstaðir. The bacteria culture is different, the acidity is both milder and more pronounced, and the texture is between yogurt and cottage cheese (betraying its designation as a cheese, not a yogurt). Don't miss out on the real skyr experience. (Egilsson, 2015)

Indeed, in Erpsstaðir as in Efstidalur – places that produce both skyr and its historical, cultural, and agricultural context – the visitor experiences the entire food supply chain from udder to ice cream, from grazing to dining, from milk to skyr, from live cultures to cultural heritage all at once. Who would have thought thirty years ago that skyr, the most quotidian of foods, would become a vector for heritage emotions? Who would have believed that milking might become a meaningful form of entertainment for people eager to observe it on a weekend outing or summer vacation?

Traditional skyr provides a powerful example of heritage as a value-added industry that works in tandem with tourism. In her theorization of cultural heritage, Kirshenblatt-Gimblett maintains that heritage adds the "value of pastness, exhibition, difference and, where possible, indigeneity" to its object. Places, goods, and practices that have lost their value, their former function or economic viability – "the obsolete, the mistaken, the outmoded, the dead, and the defunct" – undergo a transvaluation that grants them a second life as heritage (Kirshenblatt-Gimblett, 1998, p. 149–150). As such, they evoke, with more or less success, heritage emotions.

In and of itself, to make skyr is to add value to skimmed milk, a low-value byproduct of butter-making. Skyr-making turned this byproduct into a comestible and conservable source of protein while producing a preservation medium for meat in the sour whey that remained when the skyr had been strained. The Erpsstaðir Creamery is one of three producers featured in the Slow Food presidium, the objective of which is to support the producers by adding value to their product with the Slow Food label. The label is a stamp of authenticity that references tradition. It helps to distinguish traditional skyr from competing products like mass-produced, pasteurized skyr from MS Iceland Dairies while encouraging consumers to use their purchasing power to preserve traditional skyr. Indeed, above all else, Slow Food emphasizes the distinction of traditional skyr from its industrial counterpart, locating the mark of tradition in the transfer of microbial cultures from older to newer batches. Erpsstaðir's designation as an ÉCONOMUSÉE®um further helps to coagulate the values of difference, pastness, and indigeneity as part of its skyr, developing the techniques of exhibition still more in spaces of interpretation and guided tours. If skyr is a value-added byproduct of butter and ice cream, then through the work of distinction, tradition emerges as a byproduct of industrialization.

Heritage adds value to this byproduct by transvaluing its obsolescence as authenticity, playing on the heritage emotions of consumers.

It is worth noting how skyr, once a heterogeneous, local foodstuff with diverse microbial cultures and important variations in manufacturing methods from region to region and from one farm to the next, moved gradually through the twentieth century toward full standardization in MS Iceland Dairies' monopoly only to enter a new phase of localization and diversification in the first quarter of the twenty-first century. At Erpsstaðir, dairy farmer and scientist Þorgrímur started his own skyr using live cultures from mass-produced skyr (*Óhrært skyr* brand). That is to say that live cultures harvested from mass-produced skyr create a new cultural (in a double sense) context. Diversification emerges through this lens as a byproduct of standardization.

Added value comes to this byproduct from the skyr narratives that this newfound diversity and tradition enable and legitimate. MS Iceland Dairies has tuned into these stories and adopted them as its own. Indeed, the export of skyr relies on the added value of these narratives.

3.8 Cool Frame for Export

If life must be lived forwards, it can only be understood backward, in the words of Søren Kierkegaard. Before the definition of the recipe for traditional skyr and its appeal to support Slow Food and save the world, the homepage of the Slow Food Foundation for Biodiversity thus begins by tracing skyr through "time immemorial":

> Skyr, a fresh acid-set cheese made from cow's milk, has ancient origins. It was already an integral part of the diet of Iceland's first settlers over a thousand years ago, and Icelandic families have been making it at home since time immemorial. The cheese is mentioned in medieval sagas, and traces have been found during the archaeological excavation of medieval farms. (Traditional Icelandic Skyr)

Attentive readers will notice the convergence between the story of skyr as told by Slow Food and the story as told by MS Iceland Dairies as well as by the US-Icelandic skyr producer Icelandic Provisions in the quote that opens this section: "It fueled the exploits of Vikings and farmers for generations. Imagine what it could do for you!" Both appeal to consumers by anchoring skyr in a millennium-long tradition dating back to Iceland's settlement. The medieval (Viking) sagas provide a *terminus ante quem* before which skyr-making must have begun and a literary context for its marketing, as one of our interviewees made clear. A product developer at MS Iceland Dairies, Björn Sigurður Gunnarsson has taken an active part in developing skyr for international markets over a long period of time:

> One of the things we've been working with is this history of skyr and how we can create a cool frame for its export by recounting its history. We've seen, during this expansion of markets, that people are very much interested in that. People are actually quite surprised; not many know that skyr is particular to Iceland and that its history is so long, right from the beginning of settlement here ... This history and the connection to the Viking period – we can even quote the old Icelandic sagas – people totally fall for that ... We have promoted skyr widely, and at trade conferences, we have explained that it is a traditional food mentioned in several of the Icelandic sagas. We haven't analyzed it in any detail, but it is mentioned in a number of sagas.

Indeed, reference to the medieval sagas is a staple of skyr's international marketing, and not only by MS Iceland Dairies but also in advertisements and "back stories" for the skyr produced by various dairy conglomerates outside Iceland. Occasionally, two to four of the best-known sagas that feature skyr are mentioned by name, the *Saga of Egil*, the *Saga of Grettir the Strong*, the *Saga of the People of Ljósavatn*, and *Sturlunga Saga*. The marketing stops short, however, of retelling any relevant episodes from the sagas. And no wonder. The most memorable introduction to this longstanding staple of the Icelandic diet is perhaps to be found in the *Saga of Egil* set in the tenth century CE. The eponymous protagonist takes such offense at having been served skyr when his host, named Armod, had better food in the pantry that, after first quenching his thirst on strong ale, Egil

> stood up and walked across the floor to where Armod was sitting, seized him by the shoulders and thrust him up against a wall-post. Then Egil spewed a torrent of vomit that gushed all over Armod's face, filling his eyes and nostrils and mouth and pouring down his beard and chest. Armod was close to choking, and when he managed to let out his breath, a jet of vomit gushed out with it. (*Egil's Saga*, 2004, p. 156)

Not exactly the darling of marketing departments. After a breather, Egil sat back down and asked for another drink, blaring out in verse: "With my cheeks' swell I repaid / the compliment you served" (156). In other words, he was displeased with the hospitality and sent the meal back. Perhaps the least flattering review of skyr from any age, it comes as no surprise that this account does not feature in any skyr advertisements we have come across.

The same goes for the *Saga of Grettir the Strong* set in the eleventh century CE, in which a fellow called Audun is carrying skyr curds in a skin pouch back from his remote summer dairy when Grettir the Strong deliberately trips him up: "Audun bent down to pick up the curd pouch, slung it into Grettir's arms and told him to take what he was given. Grettir was covered with curds, which he considered a greater insult than if Audun had given him a bloody wound" (*The*

Figure 26 Archeological skyr. Remains of ancient skyr excavated in 1883 at Bergþórshvoll, the principal farm in the Saga of Njál. These remains were shown as part of the 2024 exhibition "Microbes in the Home" in Iceland's Museum of Design and Applied Arts. Photograph by Stúdíó Fræ. Courtesy of Iceland's Museum of Design and Applied Arts.

Saga of Grettir the Strong, 2005, p. 67). In *The Saga of the People of Ljósavatn*, a dubious character called Þorbjörn rindill (Thorbjorn "pip-squeak") hastily gobbles up a meal of runny skyr and soon thereafter meets his fate when an enemy plunges a spear into his bowels. In what appears to be the saga's idea of a joke, the skyr spurts out of his body and onto his killer (The Saga of the People of Ljósavatn, 1997).

Finally, in *Sturlunga Saga* as part of a vendetta, a party of men burns down the house of a powerful chieftain, Gissur Þorvaldsson, killing his wife and three sons. Meanwhile Gissur narrowly escapes by taking refuge for hours in a barrel of sour whey, hidden behind a barrel of skyr in the farm's skyr storage room – instead of coming out of the house and facing his adversaries like a man, in the mold of saga heroes (*Sturlunga Saga*, 1970). In all four cases, skyr in the sagas is thus a medium of shame, so to speak: of vengeance, insult, ridicule, and dishonor. It seems likely, moreover, that the shamefulness of being covered in skyr (or its residue, whey, in the case of Gissur) has to do with the feminine connotations of dairying; recall the words of Anna Sigurðardóttir that it was not until well into the twentieth century that men in Iceland no longer found it disgraceful to milk a cow (Sigurðardóttir, 1985, p. 248). In effect, these medieval men are all feminized by their enemies (Figure 26).

3.9 Exporting Skyr, Exporting Women

The majority of skyr advertisements – whether from MS Dairies in Iceland, Icelandic Provisions in the USA or European competitors such as Arla – highlight skyr making as women's heritage, passed from mother to daughter for a millennium or more. It was the women who safeguarded traditional knowledge to produce skyr as well as the genetic resources – the right composition of the fermented microbial communities – needed to sustain continuous skyr making. These ads typically reference Icelandic nature and strong Icelandic women, often wearing wool sweaters (Figure 27).

One of our favorite advertisements for skyr is a TV ad from Arla. It features a gainly Icelandic woman in a wood cabin with rugged mountains in the background. Wearing a traditional wool sweater, she looks up from her jar of skyr to ask Dutch viewers (in Icelandic with Dutch subtitles): "What is this?" She explains that skyr is nothing new, that it has been around for a thousand years. It is neither yogurt nor quark, she adds, emphasizing the uniqueness of Icelandic skyr. Without further ado, she gets up, steps outside, and sets to work cleaving wood with a large ax as the Dutch narrator's voiceover introduces this fat-free, protein-rich superfood (Arla skyr, 2015). Behind her is a big pile of split logs; it's been a busy week. The message of strength, vigor, and woman power could hardly be less oblique. As a sidenote, we find the wood cleaving particularly amusing; Iceland is known for its lack of trees and therefore has no tradition of warming up houses with wood. This illustrates well Vittersø and Amilien's distinction between local and localized food, with locality, culture, and tradition thrown in as "added values" for the latter (Vittersø and Amilien, 2011).

In another television ad from Arla aimed at the German market, the opening frame shows a buoy floating in the sea against a background of snowcapped mountains. A light comes on in a solitary house on the coast. Inside the house, we see a woman named Hildur, who has just woken up and is preparing for her

Figure 27 Women in wool sweaters start their day with Arla skyr in the rugged landscapes of Iceland. Courtesy of Arla Foods Netherlands.

daily swim in the sea. Before diving into the cold ocean, she needs a hearty breakfast: Arla skyr. "This is our old family tradition, the morning swim," the German narrator tells us, adding that skyr is fat free and rich in protein. Hildur then dives from the dock and swims "to the buoy and back," precisely as her mother did before her every morning. Hildur's daughter, dressed in a traditional Icelandic wool sweater, watches her mother with admiration from the kitchen window. Swimming in the cold sea, the narrator continues, is something that Hildur would like to pass on to the next generation. The ad closes with a shot of three generations: Hildur and her daughter, while Hildur holds a photo of her mother on the dock coming up from the sea after swimming "to the buoy and back" (Arla Skyr, 2017).

Arla is a multinational dairy company based in Sweden and Denmark, but it sells its products in Europe and beyond – it is the fourth-largest dairy company in the world, and these are just two of its many skyr ads featuring strong Icelandic women, lots of wool, and Arla skyr. While MS Dairies has a much smaller advertising budget, its ads are equally gendered and dominated by similar visual motifs.

It is apparent from these advertisements that the chief target consumer group for skyr are women who recognize themselves in the ads: radiating health and happiness, they couple strength with beauty. It is well established that women consume more so-called superfoods than men (Franco Lucas et al., 2021; Kirsch et al., 2022; Siró et al., 2008) and "superfood advertorials are overwhelmingly targeted to women" (Sikka, 2017, p. 93). Indeed, as Tina Sikka notes, "superfood marketing has come to frame its products as not only a means through which to attain the ideal body type ... but also a source of nutrition and energy needed for women to take on the busy, multitasking, caretaker roles they have traditionally been associated with" (Sikka, 2017, p. 94). From dairy maids to superwomen, the marketing thus instrumentalizes mother cultures in more than one sense of the term.

3.10 Heritage Branding

As noted in the previous section, in 2017 MS Iceland Dairies promoted Ísey skyr, a new brand for export, referencing Iceland itself in the guise of a woman and 1100-year skyr making tradition in Iceland. What is noteworthy about the skyr narrative that MS Iceland Dairies promotes is its similarity to the one recounted by Slow Food. MS Iceland Dairies, by its own account, builds on this historical legacy. And it is true that there is no denying the lineage.

Historically, however, it is also clear that the creation of the dairy farmers' cooperatives in the twentieth century and the ensuing industrialization of production spelled the end of the very tradition that MS Iceland Dairies claims as its own: the end of traditional skyr-making on individual farms; the end of traditional variation in methods, taste, and texture; the end of microbial diversity and continuity; as well as the end of skyr's traditional function in the Icelandic diet, the traditional manner of serving it, and its traditional role as a medium of preservation. With reference to the discourse of heritage, MS Iceland Dairies thus markets skyr by claiming the very traditions that it moved beyond, left behind, retired, and replaced (Figure 28).

Figure 28 A miniature at the Skyrland exhibition illustrates how men took over the dairy. Photographer unknown. Courtesy of MS Icelandic Dairies.

In its marketing in English speaking countries, Ísey skyr is a "new dairy from a timeless tradition" (New Dairy from a Timeless Tradition, 2022). In the same vein, MS Iceland Dairies' US trading partner, Icelandic Provisions, markets skyr to Americans by referencing the "long history" of skyr-making, mentioning that this deeply rooted Icelandic tradition is believed to have remained unchanged from first settlement until the middle of the last century. In case their niche audience isn't paying attention, they persist: "Icelandic Provisions is the only authentic Icelandic Skyr brand in the United States that uses heirloom Icelandic Skyr cultures and a recipe that dates back thousands of years" (About us, 2025).

Why this sudden emphasis on history, tradition, and heritage? We asked Björn Sigurður Gunnarsson at MS Iceland Dairies, who has been active in developing skyr for international markets. According to Björn, Ísey Skyr is simply a rebranding of Skyr.is – the "new generation" of skyr from 2001 – without any notable changes to the product itself. Skyr.is arrived on the scene at the time of the dot.com bubble at the turn of the millennium, but by 2017, its branding was obsolete. A new marketing strategy was needed. Gunnarsson explained that referencing tradition and heritage related much better to the Zeitgeist. What matters most, Gunnarsson said, is the quality of the product, but he added that the cultural context and history help to frame skyr in terms of authenticity.

If with Nathalie Heinich, we see the value of authenticity as a correlate of heritage emotions, we may deduce that, in framing skyr in terms of its authenticity, MS Iceland Dairies is playing to these emotions: to brand skyr as heritage is an attempt to tap into the Zeitgeist. In this way, the company takes its cue from the staging at Erpsstaðir and Efstidalur, reproducing, by different means and in so far as possible, the heritage values of authenticity and presence in the mass marketing of industrially produced skyr as a way of adding value to the product.

Indeed, we observe a dialectic of scale over the past two decades, where the mergers of dairy cooperatives and the standardization of industrial skyr created a niche in the market that Þorgrímur and Helga at the Erpsstaðir creamery, and later the siblings at the dairy farm in Efstidalur, have found a way to fill. While MS Iceland Dairies branded its mass-produced skyr with the country domain ".is," Slow Food promoted traditional skyr and skyr-making farmers in response to the threat posed by standardization. In the tourism boom, skyr offers visitors a way to ingest local culture, and local skyr destinations multiply. The latest additions are the Ísey Skyr Bars located in gas stations in Reykjavík and at the international airport as well as in the Skyrland museum.

As part of its rebranding of skyr.is in 2017, MS Iceland Dairies – the industrial dairy monopoly – adopted the Slow Food narrative of skyr's history and the unbroken tradition of skyr-making through the centuries, placing itself as the legitimate heir to this legacy in a bid to distinguish its product from other brands of skyr. To quote Gunnarsson, the product developer at MS Iceland Dairies, once more:

> Skyr is a novelty that many have jumped on, as happened also with Greek yogurt ... We just have to accept that. Under those circumstances, it may be better to brand ourselves in a particular way. That's what has happened with Ísey Skyr, which also refers to its origins. We launched it in 2017, and we think it's off to a good start. It distinguishes us, but it takes some time to build a brand in a way that everyone realizes that it is the real deal.

Adopting a distinction from Virginie Amilien and Gunnar Vittersø, if we characterize skyr from Erpsstaðir and Efstidalur as local food (i.e. short traveled and with a close relationship between producers and consumers), then we might contrast it with Ísey skyr as a localized food product that is further from its origin and with more distance between producer and consumer, but with locality, "culture and tradition as added values" (Vittersø and Amilien, 2011). The two don't clash, and they don't compete for the same market share. Instead, they complement one another – their relation is symbiotic. Artisanal skyr makers even get their starters from big dairy's niche brand, *Óhrært skyr*. And conversely, the small entrepreneurs in Erpsstaðir, Efstidalur, and elsewhere pose no threat to MS Iceland Dairies. On the contrary, their existence helps validate the brand storytelling, which is designed to distinguish Ísey skyr from its foreign competitors on dairy shelves abroad (cf. Yotova, 2018, p. 49).

4 The Problematics of Cultural Heritage: Conclusions

4.1 Producing the Local for Export

After a relatively quiet life in the Icelandic diet for more than a millennium, in the twenty-first century skyr found its way into dairy aisles and advertisements from Singapore and Japan to France and the United States. Its breakthrough as a healthy superfood is partly captured in branding efforts and advertising campaigns produced in recent years for various types of skyr. It was not until skyr had become a standardized export commodity, however, that action seemed needed to protect the traditional way of making skyr in Iceland. Picking up on the "heritagization" pioneered by Slow Food and by small farmers catering to tourists, industrial skyr producers too have come around to narrating the cultural history of skyr, employing heritage branding to carve out a unique place within the global dairy-scape. Indeed, one might say that the cultural history of skyr is an incidental, secondary product of its industrialization and export.

Regardless of where they are located, skyr producers reference Icelandic landscapes, culture, and history in the marketing and packaging of their skyr. Original bacterial cultures, exceptionally strong Icelandic women, traditional wool sweaters, rugged mountains, and snow-white glaciers feature prominently in what we have dubbed the "Skyr Wars," conducted on screen, in the dairy aisle of your supermarket, as well as in courtrooms and lawyers' offices. We argue that legal skirmishes over skyr in the past two decades, including trademark claims to the word skyr, the certification of skyr cultures, and legal challenges to the ways in which skyr is marketed with reference to heritage and origins, are ways in which ownership over skyr – or skyr sovereignty – is asserted, confirmed, and rejected, always with reference to its history and its definition as cultural heritage.

Drawing on Carl Schmitt's notion of sovereignty as the exception to rules (Schmitt, 2005 [1922]) and on Giorgio Agamben's argument that sovereignty is indistinguishable from a permanent state of exception (Agamben, 1998), Hafstein and Skrydstrup (2020) have argued elsewhere that cultural property is a technology of sovereignty. The use of trademarks and other rights-based claims to assert exclusive property rights in the name skyr – "the right to name it and the right to police its boundaries" (Grassoni, 2017, p. 29) – claim precisely such exception to free market rules in the name of cultural history. As the case of

Icelandic skyr demonstrates, however, the local or national may also be closely intertwined with private, corporate interests.

It is tempting to consider skyr from the perspective of "culinary nationalism," a concept coined "to refer to pride in the distinctiveness and quality of one's cuisine being transferred to pride in the nation itself" (Long, 2021, p. 6). However, we have resisted that temptation as we believe that if skyr has acquired symbolic significance as a national heritage food, the making of its national identity is not so much a political project as a carefully considered marketing strategy. Foregrounding of skyr's Icelandic origins and identity represents an attempt to "enrich" or add value to a product in domestic and international markets through national branding: capitalism before nationalism.

In 2021, a class action lawsuit was filed against Icelandic Provisions. The charges: misleading consumers about the place of origin of the product (produced in upstate New York) while exploiting their desire for authenticity and their wish to maintain local traditions and cultures. Specifically, the plaintiffs alleged:

1. Icelandic Provisions, Inc. ("defendant") markets, manufactures, labels, distributes, promotes and sells the traditional Icelandic dairy product – "skyr" – under the Icelandic Provisions brand ("Product").
2. Defendant's marketing and advertising of the Product gives consumers the impression it is made in Iceland, including its front label representations of "Traditional Icelandic Skyr," "Icelandic Provisions" and the image of the Icelandic countryside with a snow-covered backdrop.
3. However, the Product is not made in Iceland but in upstate New York.
4. In marketing and advertising its Product to give the impression it is made in Iceland, Defendant understands that today's consumers are faced with a dizzying area [sic] of products and choices.
5. For many consumers, "authenticity has overtaken quality as the prevailing purchasing criterion."
6. Consumers are willing to pay a price premium "for what they perceive to be authentic products, particularly those perceived to be authentically associated with a specific place," often where the product originated.
7. Examples of these products include Scotch whisky from Scotland, maple syrup from Vermont, tomatoes from Italy, chocolate from Switzerland and skyr from Iceland.
8. The reasons include (1) an expectation that a product made in the location where it was first developed will be higher quality than elsewhere and (2) a desire to support and maintain local traditions and cultures at the expense of large-scale production by international conglomerates.

...

41. Had plaintiffs and class members known the truth, they would not have bought the Product or would have paid less for it.

42. The Product is sold for a price premium compared to other similar products, no less than $1.99 for 5.3 oz cup, higher than it would otherwise be sold for absent the misleading representations.

. . .

72. Plaintiffs and class members desired to purchase skyr that was made in Iceland and believed they were doing [that] and relied on Defendant's representations, omissions and half-truths. (Mantini and Trezza v. Icelandic Provisions, Inc.)

In other words, the lawsuit alleges that the heritage branding of skyr is a complete success. Heritage branding thus seems to offer a competitive advantage (Yotova, 2018). It also adds value to a product with a relatively high price tag compared to other products on the same dairy shelf (Lien, 2003, p. 165). Sales suggest that this is a successful branding strategy for skyr.

Incidentally, the same law firm (Sheehan & Associates, P.C., Great Neck, NY) that launched the complaint against Icelandic Provisions also filed a nearly identical class-action complaint against Heineken USA two months earlier. The latter lawsuit takes Heineken to task for marketing beer imported from the Netherlands – not from Mexico – as "Original Tecata Cerveza": "Today's consumers are faced with increasing commercialization of products and seek brands that are genuine–Mexican beer from Mexico, Italian tomatoes from Italy, etc." (Schelmetty et al. v. Heineken USA, Inc.). It seems that Sheehan & Associates, too, have found a niche with interesting prospects in the field of cultural authenticity and heritage branding. The lawsuit against Icelandic Provisions, however, was dismissed by a federal court in January 2022.

4.2 Byproducing Culture(s)

For our purposes, what is most illuminating about these lawsuits is the (feigning of) cultural naiveté on which these claims rest. By taking heritage branding at face value, Sheehan & Associates help us understand the work that heritage does and to untangle the messy relations it involves between local and global. We find Barbara Kirshenblatt-Gimblett's analysis of cultural heritage helpful in this context. She describes heritage as a value-added industry; in harnessing history to contemporary ends, cultural heritage gives "the obsolete, the outdated, and the defunct" a second lease on life as a representation of itself. Such representations are neither neutral nor innocent. They do work in the world: rearrange social relations, generate new consciousness, and revise economic rationales. The heritagization of skyr is a rich example of such reorchestration of the social and the economic under the sign of cultural heritage.

As we have shown, the staging of locality and authenticity in skyr exhibitions and tourist productions in Iceland is integral to the branding of skyr in global markets. Moreover, the case of skyr also helps us understand heritage branding as a reinterpretation of industrialization. If the dairy industry has transformed the production of skyr in pursuit of standards, time, and scale, the branding of industrial skyr as cultural heritage (in a dual sense) transforms its meaning, engendering historical consciousness and local identity. To be more exact, these come about as value-added byproducts of its marketing and export.

In one sense, skyr has always been a value-added byproduct. Butter was a highly valued product in Iceland's pastoral economy in past centuries. Butter could pay rent and it could pay wages. Once the cream for the butter was skimmed off the top of the milk, however, that left nine liters of skimmed milk for every liter of cream as a low-value byproduct of butter. To make skyr was to add value to this byproduct, preserve it, and make a protein-rich staple. In a parallel fashion, in a post-industrial agricultural economy that relies on tourism, the production of ice cream in Erpsstaðir and Efstidalur leaves skimmed milk, out of which farmers create old-fashioned country skyr for added value. In other words, skyr is a value-added byproduct of butter (and ice-cream) making.

Thanks to the work of distinction that Slow Food pioneered, we argue, tradition is likewise a byproduct of industrialization. By transvaluing as markers of authenticity those dairying techniques rendered obsolete by industrialization, cultural heritage adds value to this byproduct. As we have seen, the dairy farmer at Erpsstaðir used live cultures from mass-produced skyr as a starter for his homemade skyr. Cultures harvested from mass produced skyr thus helped to create a new cultural context. It follows, then, that diversification is a byproduct of standardization.

Finally, as part of its branding for international markets, as well as the domestic one, storytelling about skyr's history in Iceland highlights its local identity, staged not only on a handful of farms but also in Skyrland in Selfoss, a recreated historical building with a multimedia exhibition catering to all the senses, designed to domicile skyr in Iceland as part of its international marketing. That is to say that the case of skyr illustrates local identity as a value-added byproduct of export.

All told, if skyr-making adds value to skimmed milk, then it holds equally true that heritagization adds value to skyr. The transformation of skyr from a modest staple to heritage stardom demonstrates how emotion adds value to contemporary food branding. Key to this transformation is the sharing of heritage emotions, which brings people together in different social contexts such as at dairy farms and in Skyrland, as well as through marketing and advertising. Only a pinch of old skyr is needed to produce a new batch of heritage emotions that relate to values of authenticity, connecting producers and consumers, the past and the present, and products and places. To taste skyr is to do emotion in a way that moves people across time and space.

Further, we maintain that there is a more general lesson in the analysis we propose of the empirical example of skyr; it demonstrates how local and global practices mutually shape one another in a discourse of heritage. The heritagization of skyr aligns the dairy product with international trends and markets while re-orienting people's thoughts and actions on a domestic level. This re-orientation places skyr in a new cultural context that changes how Icelanders relate to their own food culture, creating a double vision of sorts, in which skyr is discursively reframed as cultural heritage – authentic and extraordinary – while simultaneously remaining the most ordinary and unremarkable of breakfast staples. This heritagization stages the production and consumption of Icelandic skyr as heritage even as its general consumption remains offstage on the kitchen table. The performance of locality, history, and cultural context on the heritage stage facilitates skyr's heritage branding, which helps to move it through global spaces of consumption.

4.3 Inventing Cultures, Inverting Skyr

The story of skyr is simultaneously the story of the longstanding symbiotic relation between microbes and women in the preindustrial dairy. However, as we have witnessed, this relationship changed dramatically during the past century. Analyzing the trajectory of skyr making in the past and the present, we argue that a double inversion is involved in the transformation of skyr from traditional food to contemporary heritage commodity. The first inversion involves gender. Industrial dairies moved dairying out of a female domain and into a male social and economic order (that of industrial capitalism), led by male managers and scientists, subordinating women in the dairy and reinterpreting their contribution as unskilled labor. Deprecation of women's work and depreciation of its value is an integral part of the legacy of modern skyr production (Figure 29). In contemporary branding and marketing of skyr, however, that legacy is turned inside out as the role of women in skyr making through the centuries is narrated and celebrated. We suggest that this selective storytelling gives itself away in the way that its historical reference to women as producers of skyr in fact envisages women as consumers of skyr: superwomen who purchase superfood as heirs to farm mistresses and dairymaids who made skyr to feed the household.

Figure 29 Photograph by Bárður Sigurðsson. Courtesy of the National Museum of Iceland.

The second inversion involves the microbiome. Up until the twentieth century, skyr making fostered and relied on cultural diversity at the microbial level, which in turn fostered diversity in the taste and texture of skyr. It was made in different environments (themselves with various fermentative microbiomes), with different methods and equipment, using different types of milk with varied microbial flora in an old batch of skyr that was used as inoculum to start a new batch. De-localization (as households stopped making their own skyr), standardization, hygiene regulation, and technological innovations in the twentieth and twenty-first centuries greatly impoverished skyr's microbial diversity at the strain level. DNA analysis of cultivated microbial communities from skyr with different origins confirms this. Ultimately, the skyr-making process was radically transformed by doing entirely away with the transmission of live cultures from one batch of skyr to the next. Ironically, it was only once this transmission had been replaced with industrially produced, single-use, isolated bacterial strains that it became central, first, to Slow Food's definition of traditional skyr, and then, counter-intuitively, to the industry's definition of original and authentic "heirloom cultures" and the branding of Icelandic skyr.

The first and second inversions complement one another. In the move from the most local source of sustenance in subsistence farming, produced and consumed on the farm, to global dairy stardom, export and advertising, women as producers of skyr have been reimagined as women who consume skyr: a market niche for naturally fat-free superfood. At the same time, in the same move, the skyr cultures themselves are rebranded as "original and authentic" through their stabilization, cloning, and freeze-drying. There's a consistent and perverted logic at play here, culminating in the heritage branding of the same symbiotic relationship between women and skyr cultures to which it has effectively put an end. Who ever claimed that capitalism has no sense of humor?

4.4 A Problematic Relationship

We believe the story of Icelandic skyr also offers broader lessons about cultural heritage as metacultural production and about its relationship with capitalism, a relationship seldom analyzed in depth in the scholarly literature. In our reading, the trajectory of skyr from (a) subsistence farming and microbial diversity to (b) industrial production and standardization and then to (c) global commodity and monoculture offers an instructive study in how consumer capitalism can instrumentalize its own residue (i.e. practices and stuff that it has rendered obsolete and outmoded) under the sign of cultural heritage, in order to create market niches, to diversify production and distinguish products on a global market.

We are tempted to invoke in this context Schumpeter's classical theory of capitalism as "creative destruction" (1950), but with a twist. Out with the old, in with the new ... but also, out with old, in with the invocation of the old: the new in the guise of the old. The never-ending innovation mechanism, to which Schumpeter referred as "the essential fact about capitalism," incessantly destroys old structures and production processes while ceaselessly creating new ones (1950, p. 83). But under the sign of cultural heritage, as we have seen in the case of Icelandic skyr, that mechanism destroys traditional modes of production only to reinvent them as their own representations.

In their theorization of the shifting dynamics of capitalism in the last half-century, Luc Boltanski and Arnaud Esquerre analyze what they call the "enrichment economy," which is "based less on the production of new things than on an effort to *enrich* things that already exist, especially by associating them with narratives" (Diaz-Bone 2023, p. 2). They argue that "enriched objects" are a hallmark of contemporary trends in capitalism, adding that "any object can be enriched," through narratives that associate them with "differences and identities, which are primary resources of enrichment economies" (Boltanski and Esquerre 2016, p. 35). The rise of cultural heritage in precisely the historical period to which they refer is a prime example of this powerful strategy of narrativization that enhances the value of goods and places. "The heritage brand," they write "can now be stamped on buildings, monuments or whole districts ... often involving fabrication of more or less fictional histories" (Boltanski and Esquerre 2016, p. 34). The marketing of skyr offers an interesting illustration of the dynamics of the "enrichment economy," narrating the cultural history of skyr so as to build brands, occupy space on tightly packed dairy shelves, and move products globally. However, whereas Boltanski and Esquerre seek to distinguish value production in post-industrial societies ("enrichment economies") from the logic of industrial mass production, the case of skyr suggests that industrial products too can be "enriched" in much the same way as works of art or built heritage.

In fact, as European Ethnologist Hermann Bausinger suggested long ago, representations of traditional culture tend to invoke "the stamp of tradition ..., the artificial patina, and the presumption of wholeness and originality" (1986 [1966], p. 121), regardless of whether such representations are celebratory or critical, lay or professional, academic, curatorial, or, indeed, commercial. In the decades since Bausinger presented his critique of the criticism of "folklorism" (a term once used to describe the recycling of traditional culture out of its original context, often in new commercial or nationalistic contexts), the concept of cultural heritage has subsumed such representations of tradition under its umbrella. We tend to assume "cultural heritage" has been around forever; in fact, it is a modern coinage, and its current ubiquity is limited to the last few decades (Bendix, 2000; Hafstein, 2012; Kirshenblatt-Gimblett, 1998; Klein, 2006; Lowenthal, 1998). Over the past half-century, a vast and ever-growing number of social actors have seized upon the concept of cultural heritage in hundreds of thousands of scattered places. Those actors are public and private, individual and corporate – museums but also entrepreneurs, local cultural animators but also corporations, including dairy companies on the global market.

It is worth noting for our purposes that the rise of cultural heritage in the last quarter of the twentieth century and the first quarter of the twenty-first coincides with the transition of the global north from industrial to post-industrial, consumer societies. "Fewer and fewer people in contemporary capitalism work at making things," as Alan Tomlinson writes, while "more and more people work to make impressions" (1990, p. 21). We might describe the heritage sector as an industry of impressions – or representations. However, the postindustrial work of making impressions need not replace more industrial modes of production; the two complement one another or merge in the marketing of mass-produced "enriched" goods such as skyr.

The concept of cultural heritage defines particular relations to the objects and expressions that it describes. Its novelty speaks of contemporary societies and to their own understanding of themselves, their past, present, and future (Eriksen, 2014; Holtorf, 2012). Valuing a building, a ritual, a monument, or a dance as cultural heritage is to reform how people relate to their practices and their built environment, it is to infuse this relationship with heritage emotions such as appreciation, pride, and responsibility, it is to invoke heritage values such as authenticity, presence, and proximity. This reformation takes place through the forms of display everywhere associated with cultural heritage: from the list to the festival, not to omit the exhibition, the catalog, and the website. Kirshenblatt-Gimblett refers to these as metacultural artifacts (1998 and 2006): cultural expressions and practices (e.g. lists and festivals but also advertisement and packaging) that refer to other cultural expressions and practices (carpet weaving, ritual dance, skyr making) and give the latter new meanings (tied e.g. to locality, nationality, diaspora) and new functions (such as e.g. attracting tourists, orchestrating difference within states, or selling commodities).

A hallmark of heritage, again following Kirshenblatt-Gimblett, is "the problematic relationship of its objects to the instruments of their display" (1998, p. 156). This study brings those problems into view; we have summarized them as a double inversion. As our argument also makes evident, commercial representations of cultural heritage are in this regard not fundamentally different from other uses of heritage. In fact, as we have shown, heritage branding employs conventional heritage genres (exhibitions, websites, and festivals) but also adds such genres of display as advertisements and consumer packaging. Much like other heritage productions, the metacultural artifacts of heritage branding conjure up heritage emotions in addressing their audience; the principal difference is that they address that audience as consumers. We have seen how commercial uses of heritage can appropriate non-commercial heritage practices, as in the dairy industry's appropriation of "heirloom microbes" from fermentation enthusiasts or its assimilation of Slow Food's narrative of skyr-making traditions. But instead of censuring these appropriations as parasitic, we have shown that they belong to a symbiotic relationship between big dairy and artisanal producers. Consequently, rather than regard heritage branding and heritage safeguarding as dichotomous, we point to the common logic that unites them. We believe that the creamy case of Icelandic skyr offers a lesson in cultural heritage beyond Iceland, beyond dairy, and beyond microbiomes. A lesson in the relationship between objects described as cultural heritage, the genres of display that describe them as such, and the social actors who so describe them: a lesson in the problematics of cultural heritage broadly conceived.

References

"About us." (2025). *Icelandic Provisions.* www.icelandicprovisions.com/our-story.

Agamben, Giorgio (1998). *Homo Sacer: Sovereign Power and Bare Life.* Stanford: Stanford University Press.

Allentoft, Morten E., Martin Sikora, Karl-Göran Sjögren, et al. (2015). "Population Genomics of Bronze Age Eurasia." *Nature* **522**(7555), 167–172. https://doi.org/10.1038/nature14507.

Amilien, Virginie, Hanne Torjusen, and Gunnar Vittersø (2005). "From Local Food to Terroir Product? – Some Views About Tjukkmjølk, the Traditional Thick Sour Milk from Røros, Norway." *Anthropology of Food* **4**, 1–42.

"Ark of Taste." *Slow Food.* www.fondazioneslowfood.com/en/what-we-do/the-ark-of-taste/.

"Arla skyr." Posted 2015 by Arla Nederland. YouTube, 32 seconds. www.youtube.com/watch?v=Vr8P28_25og.

"Arla Skyr-TV-spot 2017-Was Hildur Bewegt." Posted 2017 by Arla Deutschland. YouTube, 1 minute, 21 seconds. www.youtube.com/watch?v=hYuEvTLekZI.

"Artisans at Work." (2025). https://artisansaloeuvre.com/en/about/.

Barad, Karen (2003). "Posthumanist Performativity: Toward an Understanding of How Matter Comes to Matter." *Signs: Journal of Women in Culture and Society* **28**(3), 801–831.

Bausinger, Hermann (1986[1966]). "Toward a Critique of Folklorism Criticism." In James Dow and Hannjost Lixfield, eds., *German Volkskunde: A Decade of Theoretical Confrontation.* Bloomington: Indiana University Press, pp. 113–123.

Bendix, Regina (2000). "Heredity, Hybridity, and Heritage from One Fin-de-Siècle to the Next." In Pertti J. Anttonen, ed., *Folklore, Heritage Politics, and Ethnic Diversity.* Botkyrka: Multicultural Centre, pp. 37–54.

Benezra, Amber (2020). "Race in the Microbiome." *Science, Technology, & Human Values* **45**(5), 877–902.

Benezra, Amber, Joseph DeStefano, and Jeffrey I. Gordon (2012). "Anthropology of Microbes." *Proceedings of the National Academy of Sciences of the United States of America* **109**(17), 6378–6381.

Bernharðsson, Eggert Þór (2015). *Sveitin í sálinni: Búskapur í Reykjavík og myndun borgar.* Reykjavík: JPV.

Blaser, Martin (2014). *Missing Microbes: How Killing Bacteria Creates Modern Plagues*. New York: Henry Holt and Company.

Bloomfield, Sally F. (2016). "In Future We Are Going to Have to View Our Microbial World Very Differently." *Perspectives in Public Health* **136**(4), 183–185.

Blöndal, Pétur (2007). "Skyr er ekki bara skyr," *Morgunblaðið* November 18, 2007, 10–16.

Boltanski, Luc, and Arnaud Esquerre (2016). "The Economic Life of Things. Commodities, Collectibles, Assets." *New Left Review* **98**, 31–54.

Brulotte, Ronda L., and Michael A. Di Giovine (2016). "Introduction: Food and Foodways as Cultural Heritage." In Ronda L. Brulotte and Michael A. Di Giovine, eds., *Edible Identities: Food as Cultural Heritage*. New York: Routledge, pp. 1–27.

Castillo-Castillo, Yamicela, Oscar Ruiz-Barrera, M. Eduviges Burrola-Barraza, et al. (2016). "Isolation and Characterization of Yeasts from Fermented Apple Bagasse as Additives for Ruminant Feeding." *Brazilian Journal of Microbiology* **47**, 889–895.

Chuong, Kim H., David M. Hwang, D. Elizabeth Tullis, et al. (2017). "Navigating Social and Ethical Challenges of Biobanking for Human Microbiome Research." *BMC Medical Ethics* **18**(1), 1–10.

de la Peña, Carolyn (2013). "Thinking through the Tomato Harvester." *Boom: A Journal of California* **3**(1), 34–40.

Diaz-Bone, Rainer (2023). "An Interview with Luc Boltanski and Arnaud Esquerre on Enrichment: A Critique of Commodity." *Theory, Culture & Society* **40**(7–8), 1–16.

Dunn, Robert R., Katherine R. Amato, Elizabeth A. Archie, et al. (2020). "The Internal, External and Extended Microbiomes of Hominins." *Frontiers in Ecology and Evolution* **8**, 1–12. https://doi.org/10.3389/fevo.2020.00025.

Efstidalur II (2025). https://efstidalur.is/ice-cream/.

Egil's Saga. (2004). Trans. Bernard Scudder. London: Penguin.

Egilsson, Ragnar (2015). "A Visit to the Erpsstaðir Ice Cream Valley," *Reykjavík Grapevine* July 2, 2015. https://grapevine.is/icelandic-culture/food/2015/07/02/a-visit-to-the-erpsstadir-ice-cream-valley/.

Einarsson, Sigurður (1965). *Saga mjólkursamsölunnar í Reykjavík*. Reykjavík: Mjólkursamsalan í Reykjavík.

El Sheikha, Aly Farag, and Dian-Ming Hu (2020). "Molecular Techniques Reveal More Secrets of Fermented Foods." *Critical Reviews in Food Science and Nutrition* **60**(1), 11–32.

"Endurreisn Gamla mjólkurbúsins liður í markaðsstarfi MS," *Fréttavefur Suðurlands* August 8, 2018. www.dfs.is/2018/08/08/endurreisn-gamla-mjolkurbusins-lidur-i-markadsstarfi-ms/.

Eriksen, Anne (2014). *From Antiquities to Heritage: Transformations of Cultural Memory*. New York: Berghan Books.

Eriksen, Thomas Hylland (2021). "The Loss of Diversity in the Anthropocene: Biological and Cultural Dimensions." *Frontiers in Political Science* **3**, 1–10.

Fabre, Daniel, ed., (2013). *Émotions patrimoniales*. Paris: Éditions de la Maison des Sciences de l'Homme.

Ferðamálastofa (2024). www.ferdamalastofa.is/is/gogn/fjoldi-ferdamanna/heildarfjoldi-erlendra-ferdamanna.

Foltz, Lindsey (2024) "Microbial Entanglements in the Bulgarian Cellar: Control, Collaboration, and Quiet Food Sovereignty." *Cultural Analysis* **22**(2), 96–116.

Franco Lucas, Bárbara, Jorge Alberto Vieira Costa, and Thomas A. Brunner (2021). "Superfoods: Drivers for Consumption." *Journal of Food Products Marketing* **27**(1), 1–9. https://doi.org/10.1080/10454446.2020.1869133.

Gagarín (2025). www.gagarin.is/.

Gatti, Monica, Benedetta Bottari, Camilla Lazzi, Erasmo Neviani, and Germano Mucchetti (2014). "Microbial Evolution in Raw-Milk, Long-Ripened Cheeses Produced Using Undefined Natural Whey Starters." *Journal of Dairy Science* **97**(2), 573–591.

Gerbault, Pascale, Anke Liebert, Yuval Itan, et al. (2011). "Evolution of Lactase Persistence: An Example of Human Niche Construction." *Philosophical Transactions of The Royal Society B* **366**(1566), 863–877. https://doi.org/10.1098/rstb.2010.0268.

Gilbert, Scott F., Jan Sapp, and Alfred I. Tauber (2012). "A Symbiotic View of Life: We Have Never Been Individuals." *The Quarterly Review of Biology* **87**(4), 325–341.

Gísladóttir, Hallgerður (1999). *Íslensk matarhefð*. Reykjavík: Mál og menning.

Glassie, Henry (1995). "Tradition." *Journal of American Folklore* **108**(430), 396–412.

Grasseni, Cristina (2011). "Re-inventing Food: Alpine Cheese in the Age of Global Heritage." *Anthropology of Food* **8**, 1–43.

Grasseni, Cristina (2012). "Resisting Cheese: Boundaries, Conflict and Distinction at the Foot of the Alps." *Food, Culture & Society* **15**(1), 23–29.

Grasseni, Cristina (2017). *The Heritage Arena: Reinventing Cheese in the Italian Alps*. New York: Berghahn Books.

Greenhough, Beth, Cressida Jervis Read, Jamie Lorimer, et al. (2020). "Setting the Agenda for Social Science Research on the Human Microbiome." *Palgrave Communications* **6**(1), 1–11.

Grigoroff, Stamen (1905). "Study on Edible Fermented Milk: 'Kissélomléko'in Bulgaria." *Revue Médicale de la Suisse Romande*. Genéve: Libraires-Éditeurs. Librairie de l'Université.

Gröndal, Gylfi (1985). *Mjólkursamsalan í Reykjavík 50 ára*. Reykjavík: Mjólkursamsalan í Reykjavík.

Guðmundsson, Bjarni (2024). *Búverk og breyttir tímar*. Selfoss: Bókaútgáfan Sæmundur.

Guðmundsson, Gísli (1914). "Íslenzkt og útlent skyr." *Búnaðarritið* **28**(1), 1–17.

Guðmundsson, Guðmundur, and Kristberg Kristbergsson (2016). "Modernization of Skyr Processing: Icelandic Acid-Curd Soft Cheese." In Anna McElhatton and Mustapha Missbah El Idrissi, eds., *Modernization of Traditional Food Processes and Products*. New York: Springer, pp. 45–53.

Guðmundsson, Óskar (2005). *Samsala í sjötíu ár: 1935–2005*. Reykjavík: Mjólkursamsalan í Reykjavík.

Hafstein, Valdimar Tr. (2012). "Cultural Heritage." In Regina Bendix and Galit Hasan-Rokem, eds., *A Companion to Folklore*. Malden: Blackwell, pp. 500–519.

Hafstein, Valdimar Tr. (2018). "Intangible Heritage as a Festival; Or, Folklorization Revisited." *Journal of American Folklore* **131**(520), 127–149.

Hafstein, Valdimar Tr., and Martin Skrydstrup (2020). *Patrimonialities: Heritage vs. Property*. Cambridge: Cambridge University Press.

Halldórsson, Björn ([1783]1973). *Arnbjörg: Æruprýdd dáindiskvinna á vestfjörðum Íslands, afmáler skikkun og háttsemi góðrar húsmóður í hússtjórn, barna uppeldi og allri innanbæar búsýslu*. Egill J. Stardal, ed., Reykjavík: Ísafold.

Hansen, Bodil (2006). *Familie- og arbejdsliv på landet ca. 1870–1900*. Auning, Danmark: Landbohistorisk Selskab.

Harmi, Mehdi (2024). "French Cheese under Threat," *CNRS News* January 16, 2024. https://news.cnrs.fr/articles/french-cheese-under-threat.

Hawkins, Alice K., and Kieran C. O'Doherty (2011). "'Who Owns Your Poop?': Insights Regarding the Intersection of Human Microbiome Research and the ELSI Aspects of Biobanking and Related Studies." *BMC Medical Genomics* **4**(1), 1–9.

Hálfdanarson, Guðmundur (1984). "Mannfall í Móðuharðindum." In Gísli Ágúst Gunnlaugsson, Gylfi Már Guðbergsson, Sigurður Þórarinsson,

Sveinbjörn Rafnsson and Þorleifur Einarsson, eds., *Skaftáreldar 1783–1784: Ritgerðir og heimildir*. Reykjavík: Mál & Menning, pp. 139–162.

Haraway, Donna (2008). *When Species Meet*. Minneapolis: University of Minnesota Press.

Heinich, Nathalie. 2009. "L'administration de l'authenticité: De l'expertise collective à la décision patrimoniale." *Ethnologie française* **39**(3), 509–519. https://doi.org/10.3917/ethn.093.0509.

Heinich, Nathalie (2012). "Les emotions patrimoniales: De l'affect a l'axiologie." *Social Anthropology/Anthropologie Sociale* **20**(1), 19–33. https://doi.org/10.1111/j.1469-8676.2011.00187.x.

Helmreich, Stefan (2014). "Homo Microbis: The Human Microbiome, Figural, Literal, Political. *Thresholds*, **42**, 52–59.

Helmreich, Stefan (2015). *Sounding the Limits of Life: Essays in the Anthropology of Biology and Beyond*. Princeton: Princeton University Press.

Hendy, Jessica, Matthäus Rest, Mark Aldenderfer, and Christina Warinner (2021). "Cultures of Fermentation: Living with Microbes: An Introduction to Supplement 24." *Current Anthropology* **62**(S24), 197–206.

Hernández-Velázquez, Rodrigo, Lena Flörl, Anton Lavrinienko, et al. (2024). "The Future Is Fermented: Microbial Biodiversity of Fermented Foods Is a Critical Resource for Food Innovation and Human Health." *Trends in Food Science & Technology* **150**, 1–10. https://doi.org/10.1016/j.tifs.2024.104569.

Holtorf, Cornelius (2012). "The Heritage of Heritage." *Heritage & Society* **5**(2), 153–174.

Hottin, Christian (2011). "Émotions patrimoniales: Retour sur les détours d'un programme de recherches." *Livraisons de l'histoire de l'architecture* **22**, 59–86.

Ingram, Mrill (2011). "Fermentation, Rot, and Other Human-Microbial Performances." In Mara J. Goldman, Paul Nadasdy, and Matthew D. Turner, eds., *Knowing Nature: Conversations at the Intersection of Political Ecology and Science Studies*. Chicago: University of Chicago Press, pp. 99–112.

Ironstone, Penelope (2019). "Me, My Self, and the Multitude: Microbiopolitics of the Human Microbiome." *European Journal of Social Theory* **22**(3), 325–341.

"Ísey skyr: Our story" (2025). www.iseyskyr.com/our-story.

Ívarsson, Helgi, and Páll Lýðsson (2005). *Rjómabúið á Baugsstöðum 100 ára*. Selfoss: Búnaðarsamband Íslands/Rjómabúið Baugsstöðum.

Jakobsdóttir, Nanna Elísa (2015). "Ísland í auglýsingu í Bretlandi: Segir púkalegt af Arla að stela íslenskri ímynd í hagnaðarskyni," *Vísir* April 22, 2015. www.visir.is/g/2015150429698.

Jordan, Jennifer A. (2007). "The Heirloom Tomato as Cultural Object: Investigating Taste and Space." *Sociologia Ruralis* **47**(1), 20–41.

Joseph, Hugh, Emily Nink, Ashley McCarthy, Ellen Messer, and Sean B. Cash (2017). "The Heirloom Tomato Is 'In'. Does It Matter How It Tastes?" *Food, Culture & Society* **20**(2), 257–280.

Jónsdóttir, Vilhelmína (2018). "'Að fortíð skal hyggja, ef frumlegt skal byggja': Nýtt miðbæjarskipulag á Selfossi." MA thesis, University of Iceland. http://hdl.handle.net/1946/30641.

Jónsdóttir, Vilhelmína (2019). "'Ný gömul hús': Um aðdráttarafl og fortíðleika í nýjum miðbæ á Selfossi." *Saga* **57**(2), 117–151.

Júlíusson, Árni Daníel (2013). *Landbúnaðarsaga Íslands*, 2nd vol, 1st ed. Reykjavík: Skrudda.

Jönsson, Håkan (2005). *Mjölk – en kulturanalys av mejeridiskens nya ekonomi*. Stockholm: Brutus Östlings bokförlag Symposion.

Jönsson, Håkan (2013). "Chef Celebrities, Foodstuff Anxieties and (Un)happy Meals: An Introduction to Foodways Redux." *Ethnologia Europaea* **43**(2), 5–16.

Kasper, Lynne Rosetto (2013). "Heirloom Yogurt (featuring Sandor Katz)," *The Splendid Table*: *Podcast*, Episode 538. www.splendidtable.org/story/2013/07/26/commercial-yogurt-starters-degrade-but-heirloom-cultures-last-generations.

Katz, Sandor Ellix (2012). *The Art of Fermentation: An In-Depth Exploration of Essential Concepts and Processes from around the World*. Vermont: Chelsea Green Publishing.

Katz, Sandor Ellix (2011). "Fermentation as a Co-evolutionary Force." In Helen Saberi, ed., *Cured, Smoked, and Fermented: Proceedings of the Oxford Symposium on Food and Cooking, 2010*. Totnes: Prospect Books, pp. 165–174.

Kirsch, Fabian, Mark Lohmann, and Gaby-Fleur Böl (2022). "The Public's Understanding of Superfoods." *Sustainability* **14**(7), 3916. https://doi.org/10.3390/su14073916.

Kirshenblatt-Gimblett, Barbara (1998). *Destination Culture: Tourism, Museum, and Heritage*. Berkeley: University of California Press.

Kirshenblatt-Gimblett, Barbara (1999). "Playing to the Senses: Food as a Performance Medium." *Performance Research* **4**(1), 1–30.

Kirshenblatt-Gimblett, Barbara (2004). "Foreword." In Lucy M. Long, ed., *Culinary Tourism*. Lexington: University Press of Kentucky, pp. xi–v.

Kirshenblatt-Gimblett, Barbara (2006). "World Heritage and Cultural Economics." In Ivan Karp, Corinne A. Kratz, Lynn Szwaja, and

Tomás Ybarra-Frausto, eds., *Museum Frictions: Public Cultures/Global Transformations*. Durham: Duke University Press, pp. 161–202.

Klein, Barbro (2006). "Cultural Heritage, the Swedish Folklife Sphere, and the Others." *Cultural Analysis* **5**, 57–80.

Kolbert, Elizabeth (2014). *The Sixth Extinction: An Unnatural History*. London: Bloomsbury.

Köstlin, Konrad (1998). "Tourism, Ethnic Food, and Symbolic Values." In Patricia Lysaght, ed., *Food and the Traveller: Migration, Immigration, Tourism and Ethnic Food*. Nicosia: Intercollege Press, pp. 108–114.

Latour, Bruno. (1993). *The Pasteurization of France*. Cambridge: Harvard University Press.

Lederman, Josh, and Briony Sowden (2024). "Sacre bleu! Camembert and brie 'on the verge of extinction,' French scientists warn," *NBC News* March 29, 2024. www.nbcnews.com/news/world/camembert-brie-disappear-scientists-france-warn-rcna143862.

Lien, Marianne Elisabeth (2003). "Fame and the Ordinary: 'Authentic' Constructions of Convenience Food." In Timothy de Waal Malefyt and Brian Moeran, eds., *Advertising Cultures*. Oxford: Berg, pp. 165–185.

Long, Lucy M. (1998). "Culinary Tourism: A Folkloristic Perspective on Eating and Otherness." *Southern Folklore* **55**(3), 181–204.

Long, Lucy M. (2004). "Culinary Tourism: A Folkloristic Perspective on Eating and Otherness." In Lucy M. Long, ed., *Culinary Tourism*. Lexington: University Press of Kentucky, pp. 20–50.

Long, Lucy M. (2021). "Introduction: Culinary Nationalism." *Western Folklore* **80**(1), 5–14.

Lorimer, Jamie (2020). *The Probiotic Planet: Using Life to Manage Life*. Minneapolis: University of Minnesota Press.

Lorimer, Jamie (2016). "Gut Buddies: Multispecies Studies and the Microbiome." *Environmental Humanities* **8**(1), 57–76.

Lowenthal, David (1998). *The Heritage Crusade and the Spoils of History*. Cambridge: Cambridge University Press.

Lyons, Kristina M. (2020). *Vital Decomposition: Soil Practitioners and Life Politics*. Durham: Duke University Press.

Mantini and Trezza v. Icelandic Provisions, Inc., Case No. 7:21-cv-00618, U.S. District Court Southern District of New York, filed January 23, 2021.

"Markkinaoikeus/Marknadsdomstolen." (2015). *MAO:678/ 15 and MAO:948/ 15*. https://markkinaoikeus.fi/fi/index/paatokset/teollisjatekijanoikeudellise tasiat/1445490992259.html and https://markkinaoikeus.fi/fi/index/paatokset teollisjatekijanoikeudellisetasiat/1454665745751.html.

Marteinsson, Viggo Thor, Snaedis H. Bjornsdottir, Nadege Bienvenu, Jakob K. Kristjansson, and Jean-Louis Birrien (2010). "Rhodothermus Profundi sp. nov., a Thermophilic Bacterium Isolated from a Deep-Sea Hydrothermal Vent in the Pacific Ocean." *International Journal of Systematic and Evolutionary Microbiology* **60**(12), 2729–2734.

May, Sarah (2013). "Cheese, Commons and Commerce: On the Politics and Practices of Branding Regional Food." *Ethnologia Europaea* **43**(2), 62–77.

Metchnikoff, Elie (1996[1907]). *Scientifically Soured Milk: Its Influence in Arresting Intestinal Putrefaction*. Pomeroy: Health Research Books.

Metchnikoff, Elie (2004[1908]). *The Prolongation of Life: Optimistic Studies*. New York: Springer Publishing Company.

Miranda, María Isabel (2012). "Taste and Odor Recognition Memory: The Emotional Flavor of Life." *Reviews in the Neurosciences* **23**(5–6), 481–499.

Miðbær Selfoss (undated). https://web.archive.org/web/20190429175023/http://midbaerselfoss.is/husin/mjolkurbuid/.

Nancheva, Nevena (2019). "'Bacillus Bulgaricus': The Breeding of National Pride." In Atsuko Ichijo, Venetia Johannes, and Ronald Ranta, eds., *The Emergence of National Food: The Dynamics of Food and Nationalism*. London: Bloomsbury Academic, pp. 61–72.

"New Dairy from a Timeless Tradition," *dish* May 31, 2022. https://dish.co.nz/news-reviews/food-news/new-dairy-from-a-timeless-tradition.

"Ný kynslóð af skyri," *Vísir* February 13, 2001, 9.

"Nýja skyrið," *Vísir* February 28, 1969, 5.

"Nýjung í skyrgerð og skyrsölu," *Tíminn* November 15, 1968, 15–16.

Otis, Laura (2000). *Membranes: Metaphors of Invasion in Nineteenth-Century Literature, Science, and Politics*. Baltimore: John Hopkins University Press.

Ólafsson, Eggert, and Bjarni Pálsson (1975). *Ferðabók Eggerts Ólafssonar og Bjarna Pálssonar um ferðir þeirra á Íslandi 1752–1757*. Reykjavík: Örn & Örlygur.

Paxson, Heather (2008). "Post-Pasteurian Cultures: The Microbiopolitics of Raw-Milk Cheese in the United States." *Cultural Anthropology* **23**(1), 15–47.

Paxson, Heather (2010). "Cheese Cultures: Transforming American Tastes and Traditions." *Gastronomica* **10**(4), 35–47.

Paxson, Heather (2013). *The Life of Cheese: Crafting Food and Value in America*. Berkeley: University of California Press.

Paxson, Heather (2014a). "Microbiopolitics." In Eben Kirksey, ed., *The Multispecies Salon*. Durham: Duke University Press, pp. 115–121.

Paxson, Heather (2014b). "Re-Inventing a Tradition of Invention: Entrepreneurialism as Heritage in American Artisan Cheesemaking." In

Ronda L. Brulotte and Michael.A. Di Giovine, eds., *Edible Identities: Food as Cultural Heritage*. London: Routledge, pp. 29–38.

Paxson, Heather (2019). "'Don't Pack a Pest': Parts, Wholes, and the Porosity of Food Borders." *Food, Culture & Society* **22**(5), 657–673.

Petridou, Elia (2012). "What's in a Place Name? Branding and Labelling Cheese in Greece." *Food, Culture & Society* **15**(1), 29–34.

Pétursdóttir, Hólmfríður (1960). "Íslenzkt skyr." *19. júní, Ársrit Kvenréttindafélags Íslands*, 13–17.

Pétursson, Jón Þór (2013). "Eduardo's Apples: The Co-Production of Personalized Food Relationships." *Ethnologia Europaea* **43**(2), 17–29.

Pétursson, Jón Þór (2018). "Organic Intimacy: Emotional Practices at an Organic Store." *Agriculture and Human Values* **35**(3), 581–594.

Pétursson, Sigurður (1939). *Mjólkurfræði*. Reykjavík: Mjólkursölunefnd.

"Probiotics Market Size, Share & Trends Analysis Report by Product, by Ingredient (Bacteria, Yeast), by Distribution Channel, by End Use (Human Probiotics, Animal Probiotics), by Region, and Segment Forecasts, 2024–2030." (2024). Report made by Grand View Research. www.grandviewresearch.com/industry-analysis/probiotics-market.

Rafnsson, Sveinbjörn (1984). "Búfé og byggð við lok Skaftárelda og Móðuharðinda." In Gísli Ágúst Gunnlaugsson, Gylfi Már Guðbergsson, Sigurður Þórarinsson, Sveinbjörn Rafnsson and Þorleifur Einarsson eds., *Skaftáreldar 1783–1784: Ritgerðir og heimildir*. Reykjavík: Mál & Menning, pp. 163–178.

Ray, Ramesh, and Vinod Joshi (2014). "Fermented Foods: Past, Present and Future." In Ramesh Ray and Montet Didier, eds., *Microorganisms and Fermentation of Traditional Foods*. Boca Raton: Taylor & Francis, pp. 1–36.

Reichhardt, Björn, Zoljargal Enkh-Amgalan, Christina Warinner, and Matthäus Rest (2021). "Enduring Cycles: Documenting Dairying in Mongolia and the Alps." *Current Anthropology* **62**(S24), S343–S348.

Rest, Matthäus (2021). "Preserving the Microbial Commons: Intersections of Ancient DNA, Cheese Making, and Bioprospecting." *Current Anthropology* **62**(S24), S349–S360.

Rhodes, Rosamunda, Nada Gligorov, and Abraham Paul Schwab, eds., (2013). *The Human Microbiome: Ethical, Legal and Social Concerns*. Oxford: Oxford University Press.

Rosenstock, Eva, Julia Ebert, and Alisa Scheibner (2021). "Cultured Milk: Fermented Dairy Foods along the Southwest Asian–European Neolithic Trajectory." *Current Anthropology* **62**(S24), S256–S275.

Rozzi, Ricardo (2013). "Biocultural Ethics: From Biocultural Homogenization toward Biocultural Conservation." In Ricardo Rozzi, S. T. Pickett,

Clare Palmer, Juan J. Armesto, and J. Baird Callicott, eds., *Linking Ecology and Ethics for a Changing World*. Dordrecht: Springer, pp. 9–32.

"Saga Auðhumlu" (2025). www.audhumla.is/um-audhumlu/saga-audhumlu.

Salonen, Sakari (2017). "Fight over SKYR – When Proprietary Brand Turns out to Be Generic," LinkedIn October 9, 2017. www.linkedin.com/pulse/fight-over-skyr-when-proprietary-brand-turns-out-generic-salonen/.

"Samantekt um langa sögu mjólkurafurða og starfssögu Mjólkurbús Flóamanna," *Tíminn* April 1, 1973, 10–11.

Sangodeyi, Funke Iyabo (2014). *The Making of the Microbial Body, 1900s–2012* (Doctoral dissertation, Harvard University).

Sarmiento, Eric (2020). "Raw Power: For a (Micro)biopolitical Ecology of Fermentation." In Colleen C. Myles, ed., *Fermented Landscapes: Lively Processes of Socio-environmental Transformation*. Lincoln: University of Nebraska Press, pp. 301–318.

Sayes, Edwin (2014). "Actor–Network Theory and Methodology: Just What Does It Mean to Say That Nonhumans Have Agency?" *Social Studies of Science* **44**(1), 134–149.

Scheer, Monique (2012). "Are Emotions a Kind of Practice (And Is That What Makes Them Have a History)? A Bourdieuian Approach to Understanding Emotion." *History and Theory* **51**(2), 193–220.

Scheer, Monique (2016). "Emotionspraktiken: Wie man über das Tun an die Gefühle herankommt." In Matthias Beitl and Ingo Schneider, eds., *Emotional Turn?! Europäisch ethnologische Zugänge zu Gefühlen & Gefühlswelten*. Wien: Selbstverlag des Vereins für Volkskunde, pp. 15–36.

Schelmetty et al. v. Heineken USA, Inc., Case No. 7:20- cv- 09985, U.S. District Court Southern District of New York, filed November 27, 2020.

Schmitt, Carl ([1922]2005). *Political Theology: Four Chapters on the Concept of Sovereignty*. Chicago: Chicago University Press.

Schumpeter, Joseph A. (1950). *Capitalism, Socialism and Democracy*, 3rd ed. New York: Harper-Collins.

Sender, Ron, Shai Fuchs, and Ron Milo (2016a). "Are We Really Vastly Outnumbered? Revisiting the Ratio of Bacterial to Host Cells in Humans." *Cell* **164**(3), 337–340. https://doi.org/10.1016/j.cell.2016.01.013.

Sender, Ron, Shai Fuchs, and Ron Milo (2016b). "Revised Estimates for the Number of Human and Bacterial Cells in the Body." *PLoS Biology* **14**(8), 1–14. https://doi.org/10.1371/journal.pbio.1002533.

Shepherd, Gordon (2006). "Smell Images and the Flavour System in the Human Brain." *Nature* **444**, 316–321.

Sigurðardóttir, Anna (1985). *Vinna kvenna á Íslandi í 1100 ár*. Reykjavík: Kvennasögusafn Íslands.

Sigurgeirsson, Sindri (2018). "HM-skyrið í Rússlandi," *Bændablaðið* June 21, 2018, 6. www.bbl.is/media/1/bbl.-12.tbl.2018webii.pdf.

Sikka, Tina (2017). "Contemporary Superfood Cults. Nutritionism, Neoliberalism, and Gender." In Kima Cargill, ed., *Food Cults: How Fads, Dogma, and Doctrine Influence Diet*. London: Rowman & Littlefield, pp. 87–107.

Sinsheimer, Max (2018). *Microbe Farmers: How Fermentation Artisans Are Bringing Peace to the War on Microbes* (Doctoral dissertation, Duke University).

Siró, István, Emese Kápolna, Beáta Kápolna, and Andrea Lugasi (2008). "Functional Food: Product Development, Marketing and Consumer Acceptance – A Review." *Appetite* **51**, 456–467.

"Skyr – Trademark or Noun? A Real Game of Monopoly," *Euromonitor International* November 14, 2015. www.euromonitor.com/article/skyr-trademark-or-noun-a-real-game-of-monopoly.

"Skyrgerðin opnuð í Hveragerði," *Fréttavefur Suðurlands* May 13, 2017. www.dfs.is/2017/05/13/2183/.

"Skyrgerðin í Hveragerði færir út kvíarnar," *Fréttavefur Suðurlands* August 26, 2017. www.dfs.is/2017/08/26/skyrgerdin-i-hveragerdi-faerir-ur-kviarnar/.

"Skyrið verður áfram íslenskt," *Morgunútvarpið Rás 2*. November 7, 2013. www.ruv.is/frett/skyrid-verdur-afram-islenskt.

Skyrland (2025). https://skyrland.com/.

Sommestad, Lena (1992). "Able Dairymaids and Proficient Dairymen: Education and De-Feminization in the Swedish Dairy Industry." *Gender & History* **4**(1), 34–48.

Sommestad, Lena (1995). "Creating Gender: Technology and Femininity in the Swedish Dairy Industry." In Gertjan de Groot and Marlou Schrover, eds., *Women Workers and Technological Change in Europe in the Nineteenth and Twentieth Centuries*. London: Taylor & Francis, pp. 135–150.

Soudry, Yaël, Cédric Lemogne, David Malinvaud, Silla Consoli, and Pierre Bonfils (2011). "Olfactory System and Emotion: Common Substrates." *European Annals of Otorhinolaryngology, Head and Neck Diseases* **128**(1), 18–23.

Stoilova, Elitsa (2013). "From a Homemade to an Industrial Product: Manufacturing Bulgarian Yogurt." *Agricultural History* **87**(1), 73–92.

Stoilova, Elitsa (2015). "The Bulgarianization of Yoghurt: Connecting Home, Taste, and Authenticity." *Food and Foodways* **23**(1–2), 14–35.

Sturlunga Saga (1970). Volume one. Translated by Julia H. McGrew. New York: Twayne.

Tamang, Jyoti Prakash, Paul D. Cotter, Akihito Endo, et al. (2020). "Fermented Foods in a Global Age: East Meets West." *Comprehensive Reviews in Food Science and Food Safety* **19**(1), 184–217.

The Saga of Grettir the Strong. Translated by Bernard Scudder. London: Penguin.

"The Saga of the People of Ljósavatn" (1997). In Viðar Hreinsson, ed., *The Complete Sagas of the Icelanders*, volume 4, Translated by Theodore M. Andersson and William Ian Miller. Reykjavík: Leifur Eiríksson, pp. 193–255.

Tschofen, Bernhard (1998). "Cultural History Served on a Plate: Ethnicity and History as Experience and Adventure." In Patricia Lysaght, ed., *Food and the Traveller: Migration, Immigration, Tourism and Ethnic Food*. Nicosia: Intercollege Press, pp. 329–335.

Tschofen, Bernhard (2008). "On the Taste of the Regions: Culinary Praxis, European Politics and Spatial Culture – a Research Outline." *Anthropological Journal of European Cultures* **17**(1), 24–53.

Tschofen, Bernhard (2017). "'Sura Kees': An Alpine Nutritional Relic as a Ferment of Regionality." In Sarah May, Katia Laura Sidali, Achim Spiller, and Bernhard Tschofen, eds., *Taste | Power | Tradition: Geographical Indications as Cultural Property*. Göttingen: Universitätsverlag Göttingen, pp. 119–128.

Tomlinson, Alan (1990). "Introduction: Consumer Culture and the Aura of the Commodity." In Alan Tomlinson, ed., *Consumption, Identity and Style: Marketing, Meanings, and the Packaging of Pleasure*. London: Routledge, pp. 1–28.

Tómasson, Þórður (2016). *Mjólk í mat: Þættir um mjólkurstörf og mjólkurmat*. Selfoss: Sæmundur.

"Traditional Icelandic Skyr," *Slow Food Foundation for Biodiversity*. www.fondazioneslowfood.com/en/slow-food-presidia/50588/.

Tracy, Megan, and Rebecca Howes-Mischel (2018). "Gender, Microbial Relations, and the Fermentation of Food." *Cuizine: The Journal of Canadian Food Cultures/Cuizine: revue des cultures culinaires au Canada* **9**(1), 1–22.

"Um fyrirtækið" (2025). www.ms.is/um-ms/uppruninn/fyrirtaekid.

Velasquez-Manoff, Moises (2012). *An Epidemic of Absence: A New Way of Understanding Allergies and Autoimmune Diseases*. New York: Scribner.

Valenze, Deborah (1991). "The Art of Women and the Business of Men: Women's Work and the Dairy Industry, c. 1740–1840." *Past and Present* **130**, 142–169.

Valsdóttir, Þóra and Þórarinn Sveinsson (2011). "Sérstaða hefðbundins skyrs. Skýrsla Matís." Reykjavík: Matís. www.matis.is/media/matis/utgafa/10-11-Serstada-hefdbundinsskyrs.pdf.

Valsdóttir, Þóra, Eyjólfur Reynisson, Nadine Knocke, Aðalheiður Ólafsdóttir and Þórarinn Sveinsson (2011). "Hefðbundið skyr. Samanburður á heimagerðu og verksmiðjuframleiddu skyri – Forkönnun." *Skýrsla Matís 09-11*, 1–17. Reykjavík: Matís.

Vikhanski, Luba (2016). *Immunity: How Elie Metchnikoff Changed the Course of Modern Medicine*. Chicago: Chicago Review Press.

Vittersø, Gunnar, and Virginie Amilien (2011). "From Tourist Product to Ordinary Food: The Role of Rural Tourism in Development of Local Food and Food Heritage in Norway." *Anthropology of Food* **8**, 1–57. http://doi.org/10.4000/aof.6758.

Wahlqvist, Mark L. (2016). "Food Structure Is Critical for Optimal Health." *Food & function* 7(3), 1245–1250.

West, Harry (2020). "Continuity and Change in the 'Living Traditions' of Contemporary Artisan Cheesemakers." *Food and Foodways* **28**(2), 91–116.

"What is Skyr?" (2025). *Icelandic Provisions*. https://web.archive.org/web/20190508165739/https://www.icelandicprovisions.com/what-is-skyr/.

Whatmore, Sarah (2002). *Hybrid Geographies: Natures, Cultures, Spaces*. London: Sage.

Wolf-Meyer, Matthew J. (2017). "Normal, Regular, and Standard: Scaling the Body through Fecal Microbial Transplants." *Medical Anthropology Quarterly* **31**(3), 297–314.

Yong, Ed (2016). *I Contain Multitudes: The Microbes within Us and a Grander View of Life*. New York: HarperCollins.

Yotova, Maria (2018). "Ethnographic Heritage as a Branding Strategy: A Case Study of Yogurt in Bulgaria and Japan." *Global Economic Review* **47**(1), 47–62.

Acknowledgements

Over the years that we have conducted the research on which this book is based we have received help, support, and skyr cultures from a great number of people. We know we have accumulated more debts than we can account for. Nevertheless, we wish to express our gratitude to various individuals and institutions who have contributed to the data, the analysis, the arguments, and the illustrations in this book or have inspired us during its writing.

First of all, we are deeply grateful to the photo editor of the book, Sigurlaug Dagsdóttir, who has managed to find in various archives across the country some of the most beautiful photographs of dairying and skyr making. She has been very kind to put up with us. Our only regret is that we could not incorporate even more photographs featuring cows and women, a regret Sigurlaug most certainly shares.

Our thanks go to the brilliant team of the research project Symbiosis, which studied human–microbial relations in everyday life from 2020–2025 from the complementary vantage points of ethnology, folkloristics, microbiology, molecular biology, bio-statistics, nutrition science, and anthropology. At Matís Iceland Food and Biotech Company: Viggó Þór Marteinsson, Sigurlaug Skírnisdóttir, and Karla Fabiola Corral-Jara. At the University of Iceland: Áki Guðni Karlsson, Bryndís Eva Birgisdóttir, and Helga Ögmundardóttir, in addition to Bergrós Guðmundsdóttir, Birna Guðrún Ásbjörnsdóttir, Eysteinn Ari Bragason, Ragnheiður Maísól Sturludóttir, Sigurbjörg Bjarnadóttir, and Styrmir Hallsson. Many of these colleagues continue to work with us on a follow-up project on Skyr as Biocultural Heritage, which further involves Aðalheiður Ólafsdóttir, Alexandra Klonowski, and Þóra Valsdóttir, all of them at Matís Iceland. In addition, the National Museum of Iceland and Iceland's Museum of Design and Applied Arts are partners to the University and Matís in these projects; we would particularly like to thank our museum colleagues Ágústa Kristófersdóttir, Ármann Guðmundsson, Helga Vollertsen, Joe Walser, and Sigríður Sigurjónsdóttir for their cooperation and collegiality. We also would like to thank Gavin Lucas of the Institute for Archaeology, Iceland.

We dedicate this book to the memory of our colleague and former co-author, Dr. Viggó Þór Marteinsson, Professor of Microbiology at the University of Iceland and leader of microbiology research at Matís Iceland. We came up with various projects together for a period of five years, from 2020 to 2025, with topics ranging from the culture(s) of skyr to that of shark and sourdough; we are grateful for this unlikely cooperation and all that we learned from him. During the second half of this period, Viggó grappled with motor neuron disease (MND), a cruel and relentless disorder, but remained to the end committed to his research and his colleagues (we even submitted a new grant proposal together only weeks before his death). Viggó passed away while we were revising this manuscript for publication. He remains to us a source of inspiration and an exemplar of professional integrity, scientific curiosity, resolution, and courage in the face of illness and adversity.

Þorgrímur Einar Guðbjartsson and Helga Elínborg Guðmundsdóttir at Erpsstaðir Creamery have collaborated with us for many years. We would like to express sincere gratitude to them as well as to other farmers and skyr makers whom we have interviewed and who have allowed us to witness their work, including Guðrún Karitas Snæbjörnsdóttir at Efstidalur II farm, Baldur Gauti Gunnarsson at Egilsstaðabú farm, and Þorbjörg Árnadóttir at Lynghóll farm.

Moreover, we would like to thank the people at MS Dairies Iceland for their generous help in understanding the making, marketing, and branding of skyr, for giving us a guided tour of their skyr factory, and for making available to us photos from the company's rich archives: Björn Sigurður Gunnarsson, Ágúst Þór Jónsson, and Gréta Björg Jakobsdóttir. We also thank our contacts at Arla Foods, Daan Berendsen and Carol Fung-A-Loi, for their kind assistance in locating and providing us with images of Arla skyr advertisements of which we are very fond.

The book contains twenty-nine photographs illustrating the history and culture(s) of skyr making. We are grateful to the following people and institutions for their help in sourcing these photos and for allowing us to publish them here: Kristín Halla Baldvinsdóttir at the National Museum of Iceland, Kristín Hauksdóttir at the Reykjavík Museum of Photography, Hörður Geirsson at Akureyri Museum, Árný Lára Karvelsdóttir in the District Archives of Rangárvellir and Vestur-Skaftafell, Þorsteinn Tryggvi Másson and F. Elli Hafliðason in the District Archives of Árnessýsla, and Ívar Gissurarson from Nýhöfn Publishing. We also thank Guðmundur Guðmundsson for providing us with electron microscopy images taken in association with his master's thesis on skyr. Naturally, we are also indebted to the photographers, who are credited in figure captions.

For reading our earlier drafts on skyr, we thank our colleagues Alexandra Schwell, Áki Guðni Karlsson, Bernhard Tschofen, Håkan Jönsson, Kasia Herd, Laura Stark, Lisa Gilman, Monique Scheer, Ólafur Rastrick, Sigurjón Baldur Hafsteinsson, and Virginie Amilien. We would also like to thank our students, who for years have listened to us prattle on about skyr, for their patience, their interest, and their insights.

For extending an invitation to the Cambridge Element Series in Critical Heritage Studies, we are grateful to the series editors: Kristian Kristiansen,

Michael Rowlands, Francis Nyamnjoh, Astrid Swenson, Shu-Li Wang, and Ola Wetterberg. We also wish to thank the anonymous peer-reviewers for their time, their collegial generosity, and their helpful insights. The book would certainly be stronger – and longer – had we been able to follow all of their suggestions.

For encouragement and inspiration at various points when needed, each in their different ways, we raise our glasses to: Adam Bencard, Amber Benezra, Áslaug Einarsdóttir, Barbara Kirshenblatt-Gimblett, Birgitta Vinkka, Brendan Bohannan, Daniel Münster, Daniel Wojcik, Francisco Vaz da Silva, Gísli Pálsson, JoAnn Conrad, Martin Skrydstrup, Matthäus Rest, Peter Jan Margry, Regina Bendix, Salla Sariola, Sigurlaug Dagsdóttir, Tok Thompson, Veera Kinnunen, and Vilborg Bjarkadóttir.

We tip our hats to our colleagues at the Department of Folkloristics, Ethnology, and Museum Studies at the University of Iceland: Dagrún Ósk Jónsdóttir, Guðrún Dröfn Whitehead, Jón Jónsson, Júlíana Þóra Magnúsdóttir, Kristinn Schram, Ólafur Rastrick, Sigurjón Baldur Hafsteinsson, and Terry Gunnell. Takk kærlega fyrir okkur!

To our colleagues at the Department for Arts and Cultural Sciences in Lund, vi tackar så hemskt mycket: Anna Burstedt, Charlotte Hagström, Chris Martin, Gabriella Nilsson, Håkan Jönsson, Jakob Löfgren, Jessica Enevold, Karin Gustavsson, Karin Salomonsson, Kasia Herd, Kristoffer Hansson, Lars-Eric Jönsson, Lizette Gradén, Marsanna Petersen, Meghan Cridland, Michael Humbracht, Phil Dodds, Robert Willim, Susanne Lundin, Talieh Mirsalehi, and Tom O'Dell.

We would like to recognize that the research on which the book is based is one part of a larger collaborative project that was funded by the Icelandic Research Council (grant no. 218181 – 051).

Finally, we are eternally grateful to our mothers for their love, their patience, and for giving us first their microbiome, then their milk, and later lots of skyr.

Cambridge Elements ≡

Critical Heritage Studies

Kristian Kristiansen
University of Gothenburg

Michael Rowlands
UCL

About the Series
This series focuses on the recently established field of Critical Heritage Studies. Interdisciplinary in character, it brings together contributions from experts working in a range of fields, including cultural management, anthropology, archaeology, politics, and law. The series will include volumes that demonstrate the impact of contemporary theoretical discourses on heritage found throughout the world, raising awareness of the acute relevance of critically analysing and understanding the way heritage is used today to form new futures.

Cambridge Elements

Critical Heritage Studies

Elements in the Series

Heritage and Design: Ten Portraits from Goa (India)
Pamila Gupta

Heritage, Education and Social Justice
Veysel Apaydin

Geopolitics of Digital Heritage
Natalia Grincheva and Elizabeth Stainforth

Here and Now at Historic Sites: Pupils and Guides Experiencing Heritage
David Ludvigsson, Martin Stolare and Cecilia Trenter

Heritage and Transformation of an African Popular Music
Aghi Bahi

Will Heritage Save Us? Intangible Cultural Heritage and the Sustainable Development Turn
Chiara Bortolotto

The Neoliberalisation of Heritage in Africa
Rachel King

Why Historic Places Matter Emotionally: Responses – Attachments – Communities
Rebecca Madgin

In Search of National Ancestors: Heritage, Identity and Placemaking in China
Shu-Li Wang

AI and Image: Critical Perspectives on the Application of Technology on Art and Cultural Heritage
Anna Foka and Jan von Bonsdorff

A Chinese Discourse of Heritage
Song Hou

Heirloom Cultures and Heritage Branding: The Creamy Case of Icelandic Skyr
Valdimar Tr. Hafstein and Jón Þór Pétursson

A full series listing is available at: www.cambridge.org/CHSE

For EU product safety concerns, contact us at Calle de José Abascal, 56-1°,
28003 Madrid, Spain or eugpsr@cambridge.org.

www.ingramcontent.com/pod-product-compliance
Lightning Source LLC
LaVergne TN
LVHW011849060526
838200LV00054B/4245